The Burning Tower

and

Ivy

Helena Thompson
Writer
Helena Thompson is an award-winning script writer and Artistic Director of S.P.I.D. Theatre. She studied playwriting under David Edgar at Birmingham University and English at Cambridge University, and was on the National Theatre's attachment scheme. Her plays for BBC Radio 4 include *The Burning Times* (*Ivy*) (*Radio Times*' Pick of the Week) and *Superyou*. Her play *Arthur's World* (Bush Theatre) is published by Oberon. Her interactive experience *iAm* (nominated for an Offie award) toured the Arcola, Southwark Playhouse and Bush Theatre. Her plays *Bluebeard's Wives* (ICA) and *Open House* (Riverside Studios, *Time Out* Critic's Choice) are published by Plays International. Her short film *High Above the Sky* (ITV First Light Best Film Award) has won two distribution deals, three prizes and over a hundred festival screenings worldwide.

S.P.I.D. Theatre Company
Helena Thompson founded the award-winning company S.P.I.D. (Social Political Innovative Direct) in 2005 to champion high quality community theatre on council estates. The charity works on estates throughout the United Kingdom creating youth shows, professional shows, youth films and tours. Shows bring audiences together using immersive, participatory, promenade or site-specific techniques. Prizes include *Time Out* Critic's Choice, an Offie Award nomination, Fringe Report's Best Outreach Company and ITV First Light Best Film Award. Coverage includes BBC, ITV, London Live and National press.

S.P.I.D. is based in the historic Kensal House Estate ten minutes from Grenfell Tower. The charity advocates against the destruction of social housing and fights for increased investment in estates and to improve rights for those who live and work there. S.P.I.D. are proud to have raised £2.4 million to refurbish their own neglected, historic council estate community rooms.

First published in Great Britain in paperback by Methuen 2019

1

Methuen & Co Ltd
Orchard House
Railway Street
Slingsby, York, YO62 4AN

www.methuen.co.uk

Ivy was commissioned by BBC Radio 4 as *The Burning Times*
First produced as a promenade production by S.P.I.D. with
Southwark Playhouse

Methuen & Co Ltd Reg. No. 05278590

A CIP catalogue record for this title is
available from the British Library

ISBN: 978 0 413 77827 7

Typeset by SX Composing DTP, Rayleigh, Essex

Printed and bound in Great Britain by Clays Ltd, Elcograf S.p.A.

The Burning Tower

by

Helena Thompson

'Tragedy is that which is both surprising and inevitable'

Aristotle

Performances

In 2018 *The Burning Tower* toured UK estates from 31st August to 8th September. It then returned to Kensal House council estate from 11th September to 6th October for a production by S.P.I.D. in association with Bush Theatre. The acting credits for this premier are listed below.

Young people across the capital will take part in a series of estate-based performances of the play as a fundraiser to mark Grenfell's second anniversary in June 2019. Casting young unknowns alongside high profile actors will make estate voices heard, champion social housing and push for investment in these irreplaceable buildings.

The Burning Tower's development began in early 2017, when S.P.I.D. foresaw the need to dramatize the history of social housing and learn its lessons before it was too late. Originally entitled *Homes for Heroes*, it grew out of our Living History program, where local young people interviewed people from Kensal, Silchester, Grenfell, Trellick and Edenham Way about their memories of estate life. During this research, Grenfell happened and became the play's climax. The show also takes its name from a tarot card symbolising the turmoil shaking society. The play makes the case for investment in social housing and for valuing the strong community spirit at the heart of these buildings' architecture. As part of the show's creation and artistic team, we have worked with young people and residents who lost friends in the fire. The characters are inspired by those we work with.

Hannah Gittos – Director

As a director, Hannah has worked extensively for the Lyric Hammersmith. She has co-directed theatre projects in both Feltham and Rochester Young Offenders' Institute and specialises in working with socially excluded young people. She directed the multiple award winning *Womanz*, written and performed by Tessa Waters. Hannah is a founding member of the 5* sketch group Comedy Bitch, has worked repeatedly as a performer with the award-winning Tangled Feet and took her first solo show, *The Clown T & Me* to the Edinburgh Fringe festival in 2017. She has trained in Clown and Bouffon with the world renowned, Phillipe Gaulier.

Helena Thompson – Writer
Helena is an award-winning writer and Artistic Director of S.P.I.D. Theatre. Her credits include *The Burning Times* (*Ivy*) (BBC Radio 4), *iAm* (nominated for an Offie award), *Arthur's World* (Bush Theatre 2015) and *High Above the Sky*, (animated film which won the ITV First Light award).

Hayley Carmichael – The Woman
Hayley co-founded theatre company Told By An Idiot. Theatre work includes: *Crave* (Barbican), *UnderGlass* (Clod Ensemble), *First Love is The Revolution* (Soho), *Beyond Caring* (The Yard), *Too Clever By Half* (Manchester Royal Exchange/TBI), *Forests* (Birmingham Rep), *Hamlet* (Young Vic), *Fragments* (Bouffes du Nord), *Bliss* (Royal Court), *Cymbeline* (Kneehigh), *Theatre Of Blood* (NT), *Zumanity* (Cirque de Soleil), *I Weep At My Piano* (TBI), *The Dispute* (RSC), *Street Of Crocodiles* (Complicité). TV work includes: *Les Miserables, Witness For The Prosecution* (BBC), *Kiss Me First* (CH4), *Chewing Gum* (Retort). Film work includes: *Casanova* (Bluelight), *Undergods* (Scott Free) *Hunger Artist* (Daria Martin), *Tale of Tales* (Archimedes), *Emperor's New Clothes* (Bonaparte).

Alice Franziska – Em
Alice was born in Cambridge, raised in New Zealand, and eventually transported back to England aged nine. Much to her (and her father's) disappointment, she lost the accent, but she did gain a love of acting from her new county, Shakespeare's Warwickshire. Since then she has played roles including Beatrice (*Much Ado about Nothing*, SYC), Martirio (*Bernarda Alba*, Playbox) and "2" in a new piece of writing by acclaimed poet Sabrina Mahfouz (*Blame*

us for the Flood, NYT Epic stages). She has trained with the National Youth Theatre and MN Screen Academy. She is represented by Middleweek Newton.

Bianca Stephens – Sarah
Bianca trained at Royal Welsh College of Music and Drama. Theatre work includes: *A Midsummer Night's Dream* (Storyhouse), *Julius Caesar* (Storyhouse), *E15* (Lung Theatre), *The Great Austerity Debate* (Menagerie Theatre), *Always Orange* (RSC), *Blue* (Richard Burton Company), *The Rover* (Richard Burton Company), *Narrative* (Richard Burton Company), *Macbeth,* (Richard Burton Company), *In Arabia We'd All Be Kings* (Richard Burton Company), *Dogville* (Richard Burton Company). Radio work includes *Dorian Grey* (Big Finish).

Producers	Giulia James, Ursula Kelly, Olivia Lantz and Shan Rixon
Technical director	Maciej Chrzanowski
Set and costume designer	Katharine Heath
Sound designer	Tom Wilson
Operator	Charlie Snuggs
Assistant Director	Naomi Israel
Associate Designer	Montrice Henry

Thanks

The Burning Tower was inspired by S.P.I.D.'s work with council estates' residents during 2017, the year of the Grenfell fire. It grew out of *Kensington Stories*, S.P.I.D. Theatre's Living History youth project to dramatize the heritage and value of social housing. *The Burning Tower* is dedicated to all my North Kensington friends – especially Shan, Naomi, Raphael, Vassiliki, Giulia, JP and Mark.

Set

The performance is set in an estate community hall with blacked out windows. There is an exit off sight. A basic sound system is in situ. **Em** and **Sarah** have set up chairs in a circle. Around them they have set up a youth exhibition, including *Windrush* photos and a map of existing and threatened social housing. They have positioned a clock for them to check during the show. They have hung a cardboard green Grenfell heart high and prominent. They have brought with them a large wheelie suitcase containing blue tac, a first aid kit, several small electric candles, homemade snacks, and a petition to save Trellick Tower Graffiti Park.

Production

The show is one act, no interval, seventy minutes. The seating must be in the round with an exit off sight. Voices for the soundscape must be pre-recorded. Within the script, / denotes the point where the character interrupts the last person speaking. The speed of delivery is fast.

An asterisk (*) at the start of a line denotes the most important stage directions.

Characters

Em   Teenage. Speaks with street style bravado. A bit slow. Fancies herself a social activist but is actually quite nervous. She has tried hard to dress like a butch gang leader but the effect is less intimidating than she'd hoped. Unashamedly loyal, with a willingness to defend and protect her friend at any cost. Energetic. White. Talks fast, often speaking over Sarah.

Sarah   Teenage. Authentic London accent. A quick learner. Seems quite tough and no nonsense but is actually very sensitive. Cheap and understated clothes, with a hint of geek chic. Unwittingly captivating. Black/mixed race. Talks fast, often speaking over Em.

Woman   Over fifty. Posh. Well-read and intelligent. Seems opinionated and bossy but is really rather needy. Wears an old-fashioned dress that has been eccentrically accessorised to seem slightly retro or modern. Both kind and self-interested. Has a repressed energy that gradually reveals itself in a desire to move. White. Talks as easily as breathing.

ACT 1

Enter **Em**

Em Word up word up
  Gather round listen up
  Huddle in
  Living History's about to begin

  This is a show 'bout Em and Sa
  And the work we done west side
  Collecting stories far
  And wide
  Researching our past
  Estates our ends
  Chattin with neighbours
  Making new friends

  It's a show 'bout social housing
  It's a show 'bout heritage
  Estates through ages, all we share
  A show to show we really care
  It's a show for all our neighbours, it's a show to make
  new friends

It's a show from all good places, it's a show that makes
amends

This show's F'REAL! Word, this show rocks!
It's from the street! This show's a shock!
We tour the country! Spread the word!
Give all voices! Get voices heard!

* [**Sarah** *tries to clap.* **Em** *holds up a hand to stop her, gets on
the suitcase*]

Em [*ignoring her*] It's a show to make you feel!
  A show to show what's real!
  [*showing props to the audience*] Except this booze
  This booze is fake
  This spliff is too
  Chill man, woe
  No need to go
  'Chillax you cops'
  They're just our props

Sarah Can we start /now?

Em [*ignoring her*] Folks give us grief man 'cos they can
  Mouth off big time, Look away
  Get the fear, Pray and say
  'Cross the street', 'Call five oh'
  Fear and paranoia grow
  Rustle newspapers
  Cuss us mean
  Gawp at riots through a screen

Sarah [*approaching the audience*] Sorry Everyone. [*To* **Em**] /
  Em

Em [*ignoring her*] But that ain't right
  'cos them don't know
  No time to dream
  It's not what seems
  Open your eyes! And let us be
  Not the lies you see on TV!

So me and Sa come set things straight
Give you pause, make you wait
Before you judge we come inform
Kick up a storm
The lives we live
Our homes
They ain't
What some folks think
'Sink'
estates'? 'On the brink'? We're no saints
But cut some slack!
It's out of whack
To paint us 'black'?

Sarah Emma, you're not black?

* [**Em** *is wrong-footed. Gets off the suitcase. Pulls herself together*]

Em I'll do some more rapping later, yeah?

Sarah [*shaking hands with members of the audience*] I'm Sarah. I'm Living History's youth ambassador. That's the research project we'll be sharing with you folks today.

Em I'm Em. I'm an activist. Em is for mayhem. Em is for madness. Making madness, isn't it?

* [*Simultaneously,* **Em** *and* **Sarah** *each confide conspiratorially in the audience*]

Sarah I couldn't / stand Em when we first met. I'd come up Kensal with my posse, she was there in the playground, giving it all that. Oh my God, what was she like? Totally annoying. The clothes, the voice, all that OTT 'largin' it' energy?

Em Sa and I have always just clicked. I was chilling on my estate when her gang first rocked up. They weren't really my scene but oh my days, Sa and I just got each other, totally vibin', totally, total soul mates, right from the start?

Sarah Girls were giving her grief, they thought she was a /joke.

Em Her posse was well pissed that I'm so /intimidating?

Sarah They was up in her grill, she was crying her / eyes out.

Em They was jealous 'cos I'm so / popular?

Sarah She needed a mate. I hate /bullies.

Em She sent them packing. Best friends.

Sarah Best friends.

Sarah & Em From time.

* [**Em** *and* **Sarah** *fist bump*]

Em If you could all please sit your booties down?

* [*As the audience sits,* **Em** *and* **Sarah** *take up their performance positions on their suitcase*]

Sarah [*gesturing*] You'll see our display on social housing's heritage is up all around, if you've not had a chance to look, do stick around after?

Em [*aside*] You make us look *desperate?*

* [**Em** *clears her throat*]

Em Back in the day, people lived on estates that was totally shit 'cos them couldn't leave.

Sarah *Country* estates? Tied cottages? Work and board?

Em Feudal, man. Then came slums. They sucked too.

Sarah Shanty towns grew up close to the factories.

Em There was no social housing until … [*Looks to audience for help*] um …?

Sarah Philanthropy? [*To* **Em**, *annoyed*] Get it together girl?

Em [*to the audience*] I was just seeing if you guys knew …

Sarah One philanthropist really stole our hearts. Gutsy lady. Big heart.

Em Big brain.

Sarah Octavia.

Em Octavia Hill.

Sarah Over her lifetime, she bought houses here and there.

Em This map shows all social housing, including hers. [*Gestures to map of social housing*] And them what the fat cat fascists be tearing down now …

Sarah Her houses were quite far apart. She wanted tenants to / mix.

Em She wanted them part of / street

Sarah She valued community. She was big on self / reliance.

Em [*patronising*] That means taking responsibility?

Sarah Octavia paid one tenant to manage each house and report to her. Quite a battle axe, according to some sources. She spoke out on housing, social justice; the importance of history, and … [*Catches* **Em***'s eye*]

Em Is it time?

* [**Sarah** *nods.* **Em** *clears her throat*]

Em We started our interviews in 2017. Some them folks have now passed. Some them estates have now gone … This show is part of Living History.

Sarah This show is for them.

* [**Em** *switches on the music. It's a soundscape of music and news items from the Fifties.* **Em** *takes* **Sarah***'s hand, stand on suitcase. The girls close their eyes a moment, think of what's been lost. When they open their eyes, they're full of energy*]

Sarah [*bringing a hip flask of brandy from her pocket*] A flat in Octavia's Victorian house on Portobello Road.

Em These are the sounds.

Sarah The sounds of Jack's youth.

* [**Em** *strikes a carousing pose on the suitcase – drinking the brandy which* **Sarah** *passes her.* **Sarah** *goes to turn the music off*]

Em Jack's was party house 'cos he had most neighbours.

Sarah [*taking pictures of* Windrush *arrivals from the wall, all proud and hopeful and smartly dressed*] Jack's family were so brave, leaving their homes in the Caribbean. They had nothing to fall back on, but it paid off back then. They got work, and they got housed. 'Something outta nothing,' Jack said.

Em [*digging tarot cards out of her pocket*] On the boat, Jack's dad taught him magic. Could I have a volunteer please? … [**Em** *welcomes someone from the audience – she shows off*] … Please pick one of Jack's age-old tarot cards, the cards of fortune? … [*The volunteer obliges*] … Don't show me … [*Hammily showing the card at the bottom of the half pack to* **Sarah**] … Now put it back? [*The volunteer obliges*] … OK, time to watch the master … [**Em** *goes through the cards, starting at the top, dropping each one decadently on the floor*] … Man this takes talent …

* [**Em** *brings out a card, holds it triumphantly to the audience, then to the volunteer – it's a tarot card, showing a tower in flames.* **Sarah** *catches her eyes – it's the wrong card.* **Em** *quickly puts it back, keeps going through the cards. When she sees the card* **Em** *showed her,* **Sarah** *clears her throat.* **Em** *takes the next card, holds it to the audience, then to the volunteer*]

Em Is *this* your card? … [*The volunteer nods*] … Thank you, thank you! … The power of magic, the magic of history! … The magical power that unites past and present and –

* [*There's a sudden black out and the electrics fizz*]

Enter the **Woman**, *unseen*

Sarah [*in darkness*] Shit…

Em [*to* **Sarah**] You OK?

Sarah I'm fine.

Em Hello?

* [*The lights come on again*]

> *The* **Woman** *is revealed, now standing in the room*

Woman Am I too late?

Em [*she bosses*] Welcome, we've just started. Sit ya booty down, that's it …

Woman My 'booty'?

Sarah We'll just wait until you're settled.

* [*The* **Woman** *ambles slowly and arthritically towards a seat*]

Woman [*still ambling*] What have I missed, then?

Em Just some age-old, historically brilliant magic, and my awesome rap about why estates rock?

Woman Council estates?

Sarah Social housing.

Woman I'm not senile, I know what estates are! I've known this one for years! I knew its architect!

* [*Awkward silence. The* **Woman** *starts huffing a little*]

Sarah [*moving to assist*] Hold on, let me help you…

Woman I am perfectly mobile, thank you!

* [**Sarah** *halts. The* **Woman** *resumes ambling – even slower than before, still some distance from a seat.* **Em** *clears her throat*]

Em Next up: World War / One

Woman Why precisely do they 'rock'?

Em Um … what?

Woman Council estates! Keep up, you said 'they rock'!! I think I'm within my rights to ask *why*?

Sarah Fair point … we love council estates cause of Octavia Hill, [*To* **Em**] right?

Woman Octavia Hill? Wonderful woman!

Em Word. Moving /on

Woman You still haven't told me why! Come on!

Sarah [*to* **Em**] Well tell the lady? … [**Em** *motions to the clock,* **Sarah** *frowns at her*] … We love estates cause of … What magic Jack said, 'having mates nearby'? … [*The* **Woman** *motions for her to continue*] and Martin, spoken word Martin, he loved Trellick, he said he loved it … 'cos it gave him … 'something to build on'? …

Woman Yes yes, keep going?

Sarah … 'Somewhere to feel safe' …

Woman Is that all you've got?

Sarah … 'havin' people to party with' … ain't that what physics Tom said, /Em?

Em Can you please sit your wrinkly arse *down* so we can get on with the show?!

* [*The* **Woman** *halts and waits until everyone's watching*]

Woman [*leaving*] Well I *am* sorry. I thought this was a *community* show. About *history*. That *respected* age. I thought my views *mattered*; I thought I'd be *respected* and *welcomed* and *involved*. My mistake. I see I was quite wrong. Don't give me a second thought. I'm leaving as fast as I can, oh yes. Me and my 'wrinkly arse' are *out of here*, believe me.

* [*The* **Woman** *huffs more.* **Em** *rolls her eyes*]

Sarah [*to* **Em**, *sarcastic*] Nice one … [*approaching the* **Woman**] Madam, you're quite right, this show *is* for everyone … [*The* **Woman** *holds up her hand to halt her*] Estates *are* for everyone; it's in their architecture, it's in their / DNA.

Woman Are you some kind of campaigner?

Sarah [*thinking on her feet*] Right, we're campaigning to save council estates! Social housing matters, we're making the case to stop them tearing it down, aren't we Em?

Em I'm an activist?

* [*The* **Woman** *blows her nose loudly*]

Woman I don't s'pose you've thought to write this campaign down? [*When* **Em** *and* **Sarah** *look blank, the* **Woman** *turns conspiratorially to the audience*] Looks like I'm here in the nick of time … [*To* **Sarah**] … Paper and pen please?

* [**Sarah** *provides the woman with a pen and with a notebook made of pages that easily rip out, just as* **Em** *crashes a seat down loudly beside the* **Woman**]

Em Would you *please* just *sit down*?!

Woman Oh, *thank you!*

* [*The* **Woman** *is now seated at some distance from the rest of the audience.* **Em** *marches* **Sarah** *to their performance spot.* **Em** *switches on the next track. Soundscape of music and news from the Sixties. The pair step onto the suitcase, take a deep breath, close their eyes once more. When they open them, they are full of energy again*]

Sarah Outside in Clem Attlee – a concrete low rise in Fulham.

Em This garden estate was built post World War Two.

* [**Sarah** *digs out a spliff and lighter from her pocket*]

Sarah These are Tom's sounds.

Em The sounds of Tom's youth.

* [**Em** *strikes her second pose on the suitcase – smoking the joint which* **Sarah** *passes her. As before,* **Sarah** *goes to switch off the music, then re-joins* **Em** *on the suitcase*]

Em Tom's bench was best for smokin' 'cos it had most cover.

Sarah Tom had his first spliff and joined a band.

Em Tom's PM was Attlee, what founded the welfare state. Provided for those who'd fought against Hitler.

Sarah He followed Lloyd George, whose Homes for Heroes program started after the First World War.

Woman What a pig's ear those idiot men made of/ *that.*

Em Moving /on.

Sarah The point is, those guys invested in affordable / housing.

Em Not [*gesturing*] 'affordable'.

Sarah *Properly* affordable; like, five, not fifty, per cent of peoples' annual income. And respectable. Well / built.

Em [*to the audience*] Did you know that these 'luxury flats' them tear estates down for are super small? Smaller than 'homes for heroes'? And shitter? *Way /shitter?*

Woman [*interrupting and addressing* **Sarah**] Which estate are you from then?

Sarah Silchester, at the /minute

Woman Silchester … isn't that /opposite?

Sarah [*to audience*] Very few estates have any shared facilities, beyond car parks or supermarkets. And very few have lasted well. But Tom's home stood the test of time.

Em Like Tom! Perfectly preserved!

Sarah [*to audience*] Retired physics teacher. Smart guy.

Em Tom was woke, man.

Sarah He *is* woke. Who wants to give Tom a listen?

* [**Sarah** *gets the MP3 player with* **Tom**'s *recorded interview. She gives it to whichever audience member wants to listen – if no one volunteers, the* **Woman** *does. As they're listening, the show continues*]

Tom * [*recorded on the MP3*] I see what's happening ... I may be old, but I'm not blind yet [*Brief laugh*] ... I see our estates run down, people kicked out ... developers moving in ... [*mild*] ... I'm no economist, I taught physics, for my sins ... but money, the point of *money* ... isn't it, to be spent? ... To change currencies, buy different things ... but always, to be spent? ... I'm a man of science ... *rules*, I respect ... and when they *break their own rules* ... then surely ... a child could see ... the game's up?

Sarah [*to audience*] Feel free to pass Tom around.

Em [*to the audience*] If you miss a bit, just ask the person next to you to catch you up.

* [*The audience enjoys listening and passing round the headphones as the show continues*]

Woman Marvellous! More for the list ... 'Shared spaces,' yes yes, let's see ... 'places for the children to / play'...

Em 'Marvellous.' / Now

Woman Marvellous how they outlasted both the wars! A philosophy of *coexistence*!, different buildings, high and low rise, big and small! So effective at uniting different classes!

Em [*bosses the* **Woman**] Moving /on?!

Woman [*noisily blowing her nose again*] ... And always with management on site; yes! Empowering people! [*Punching the air*] 'Power to the People!' [*Encouraging others to join in*] John Lennon? ...

Sarah [*to* **Woman**, *placatory*] ... That was really fascinating, what you said about housing philosophy. It's as if you *were* Victorian./ Unfortunately

Woman Oh I'm not offended! I like to think of myself as/ ageless.

Em Look. / *Look*

Woman In some ways, I transcend time. You / see –

Em [*shouting*] Could I get a word in? … [*With exaggerated politeness, the* **Woman** *motions for* **Em** *to continue*] … It ain't that we ain't grateful, it's like, *sick* to have someone so learned / here.

Woman 'Sick'? Are you referring to my slight sniffle?

Em [*deeply disdainful*] We're paying by the hour here, Madam! What would be *sick* is if you could save up those pearls of wisdom *to the end?*!

* [*Just then, the* **Woman** *falls off her chair and sprawls on the floor. Her fall is theatrically slapstick.* **Em** *bursts out laughing.* **Em** *struggles to swallow her giggles. The* **Woman** *remains lying down, ungainly and motionless.* **Sarah** *goes to inspect her*]

Sarah … Madam?

Em [*to the audience, amused*] I reckon she just tipped herself off … [**Sarah** *jabs her in the ribs*] Ow!

Woman Excuse me? … *Excuse me?!*

* [*Someone close by – not* **Em** *– helps the* **Woman** *up – maybe* **Sarah**]

Woman Ah thank you … goodness now, oh dear … how's my hair?

Sarah Everyone, please could you check your seating?

* [*Members of the audience check their seating.* **Sarah** *helps*]

Sarah Oh no, this looks properly dodgy … this too … we'll have to cancel…

Em No no no but /Sa

Sarah We can't just go breaking health and safety?

* [*With a dismissive grunt,* **Em** *sits herself heavily down –* **Em** *lashes out at the* **Woman**. *The* **Woman** *fixes her with a look. Suddenly,* **Em** *falls off her chair and lands unceremoniously sprawling. Now it's the* **Woman** *who bursts out laughing*]

Woman [*delighted*] Oh!

Em [*livid*] You can piss right off! ... [*Awkward silence*] ... Every weekend we've been working ... and not just us, the whole group! ... talking and recording and *learning?* ... and it's been awesome! ... [*To the* **Woman**] 'til *you* with your posh *loud* mouth come fuck it all up!

Woman I see.

Em [*gesturing to* **Sarah**] She's a soft touch – she might seem tough, but she's not like me! Sa won't say it, so I'll say it for her, listen up! People think 'cos we're / *black* ...

Sarah *Em you're not / black!*

Em The point is, Sa's a *genius!* You don't know her, you don't get it, you don't get any of it! Estates is beautiful ... so beautiful, they don't even *know* ... she's doin' something real ... we're trying to *help* ... we're trying ... *trying...*

Woman [*fascinated*] What are you trying to do, dear?

Em [*shouting*] We're trying to save council estates you twat! ... [*Slowly, the* **Woman** *gathers herself and starts to walk*] ... That's right, off you toddle...

* [*The* **Woman** *sits down on the ground*]

Em Wait ... What ... ?

Woman [*to the audience*] It's very comfortable? [*To* **Em**] If they choose to stay seated, you're legally covered.

Sarah [*to the* **Woman**] ... Really?

* [**Em** *fidgets, unsure whether to be cross or relieved*]

Woman [*to* **Em**] Obviously I agree with you ... [*Despite herself,* **Em***'s intrigued*] ... These places are alive ... I feel it as much as you ... What they've done ... what they've seen ... it haunts us all ... To neglect them on purpose ... I call that unkind ... I'm with Priestley on that one ... I call that evil...

Em Wait ... Priestley? The socialist Po Po?

Sarah Em, it's *Inspector Calls?*

* [**Sarah** *switches on the next track – a soundscape of late Seventies music and news*]

Em * [*digging around in the suitcase to bring out a petition and picture to save Trellick Tower's Graffiti Park*] The top floor of Trellick Tower on Golborne Road. An iconic example of Fifties' brutalism.

Sarah These are Martin's sounds.

Em The sounds of his youth.

* [**Em** *and* **Sarah** *strike their third pose –* **Sarah** *mid signature,* **Em** *preparing to speak with passion.* **Em** *breaks it off to turn the music off*]

Sarah Martin moved in around '75.

Em He a poet.

Sarah And an artist.

Em Proper prophet, up there in his tower?

Sarah Or down Trellick's Graffiti Park.

Em Martin's graffiti was *loved*, people came from all over to check it, / til

Sarah The council wants to sell off the / park.

Woman [*interrupting, hamming it up*] What'll the bastards sell off next – our souls, our heritage, our children?

* [*The* **Woman** *notices the girls' 'brandy', ambles to take a swig*]

Em [*wrestling the 'brandy' off her*] Madam, that's a prop?!

Woman Audience participation now! [*Referring to her 'list'*] Time for the list, campaigners!

Em [*clearing her throat and gesturing for* **Sarah** *to look at the clock*] Back me up, / man?

Sarah [*to the audience*] The building was designed by architect Goldfinger. He called Trellick 'streets in the sky.'

Em His tower had tough times with gangs in the lifts and stuff, but a new caretaker put paid to all that. And the CCTV, isn't it?

Sarah Martin loved his tower's shared amen/ities

Woman If I could stop you a moment? ... [**Em** *rolls her eyes, sighing loudly*] ... Those 'tough times' – I'd imagine they were *very* bleak? Violence and aggression? No easy way out?

Em We ain't here to slag no one off?

Woman But we must face facts? Life can be extremely tough in these tall blocks of flats? Under pressure, people turn?

Em These are good people?

Sarah ... One time a TV fell past our window ... almost knocked Mum's head off ... Every day for a week ... different furniture ...

Woman It's a challenge.

Em *You're* a challenge! [*To* **Woman**] You are really *boring?*

Woman More boring than a *princess* pretending to be poor? ... [*As* **Em** *fumes, the* **Woman** *turns to the audience*] The point is, Goldfinger made some serious mistakes ... in my book, bit of a [*mimes wanking, to* **Em***'s disgust*] ... He blamed his towers' design problems on residents; when of course, people need space. Communal space ... [*To* **Em** *and* **Sarah**] Didn't the loss of surrounding land stop the fire engines / accessing ...

Sarah [*passing round the petition to save the Graffiti Park, to the audience*] We need to do the next decade now.

Em But what about Martin's spoken word? ...

Sarah [*gesturing to the clock*] Emma ...

Em You get a lot of poets round our ends. Community poets, grass-roots rappers, totally *sick* [*throwing the* **Woman** *a dirty look*] way sicker than how *some* people spraff / on?

Sarah Em when you rap on your own, it's crap!

Em I'll do it properly! [*To audience*] Listen up!

* [**Em** *closes her eyes a moment, then opens them. Temporarily, her bravado evaporates*]

Em Back in the day
 The Greeks played
 Sadness

 Always fate
 Came too late
 Acting out madness

 Now those twenty-four stories
 Cast shadows
 Long and tall

 Melancholy forewarned
 Long ignored
 Spoke tragedy for all

* [*Suddenly, all the lights go out*]

Sarah Shit … not again …

Em [*gently*] They'll come on soon, chill? [*To audience*] Stay where you are please! Don't move! We don't want any accidents!

Woman How atmospheric! Perfect!

* [*The* **Woman** *follows* **Sarah** *as she pushes the suitcase into the corner*]

Sarah Trip hazards are serious, Em … There should be an emergency light? … Are you listening?

Em OK … [*The* **Woman** *brings out a bag, removes an LED candle, turns one on –* **Woman** *cajoles the audience*] Where'd those come from?

Sarah Search me…

Woman Hands up if you'd like a candle?

Em Who's got Tom?

* [**Woman** *distributes candles to the audience.* **Em** *takes Tom back from the audience*]

Em [*aside, protects* **Sarah**] You OK to plough on?

Sarah I told you, I'm fine?

Sarah [*to* **Em**] We'll have to do without the music, though …

Em No problem.

* [*Without the suitcase in the centre of the space,* **Em** *and* **Sarah** *start to use the space more freely*]

Em [*clearing her throat*] During the Eighties, Thatcher stopped building.

Sarah She introduced Right to Buy. The bitch.

Em Sa…

Sarah You can say motherfucker, I can't say bitch?

Em [*to audience*] The point is … based on our research … magic man Jack, physics geek Tom an' crazy, brilliant Martin … the point is, loads dem *bought*? … Selling those places … 'Right to Buy'… [*To* **Sarah**] I'm not saying it was right … but it wasn't all bad?

Sarah Whatever you say, Em.

Em [*aside*] If this is about your Mum … 'bout not having bought your flat … Sa that sucks, you know I know that sucks?

Sarah Leave it, Emma … [*She swigs*]

Em The point is, special incentives …

Sarah 'Special'

Em [*to audience*] Special Right to Buy incentives made loads homeowners my ends, and it's been good! … [**Sarah** *and the* **Woman** *continue to take long swigs*] …

Em (*cont.*) mixing, like Octavia Hill said ... old and young, black and white, poor and ... [*To* **Woman**] ... *good* came out of it ... [*catches the* **Woman***'s eye*] right?

Woman Have you got any drugs? ... [*Hiccups*]

Em [*clears her throat*] ... That's it for the Eighties, folks.

Woman [*to* **Sarah**] What about you?

* [**Sarah** *smiles*]

Em [*approaching in concern*] What the ... ?

Woman I don't believe I'm alone when I say that so far, this show is a real downer.

Em Madam, we can't be getting high in / public?

Woman Oh, the law's an ass! ... [*To the audience*] ... drugs, intoxication ... the *rockbed* of neighbourly neighbourhoods! ... Alcohol's so low rent ... so depressing ... Have *you* got any drugs I could share? ... [*The audience considers*] ... I heard that today's drugs are quite nice ... I'm rather going off the booze, it makes me tearful [*the* **Woman** *hiccups*] ... but drugs ... this drug called ecstasy ... ... apparently it makes people 'loved up', sounds right up my street ... Anyone got any? ... To help me through this tedious, depressing 'entertainment', this difficult time? Little pick me up for little old 'love junky' me?

Em No we fucking haven't!

Woman 'Chill'?! [**Woman** *ambles round harassing the audience, trying to get in their pockets*] Or there's coke these days, am I right? Lots of people like coke? To be *aggressive*? [*Giggles*] 'Fuck off stop hugging me you loved up old hippy, I'm on coke!' [*To* **Em**] 'Isn't it? Isn't it?' [*To the audience*] Am I mispronouncing here?

Em Madam, you're drunk. [*To the audience*] Sorry 'bout this folks, sorry 'bout this drunken old latecomer, we will defo get a policy on this ... [*Trying to switch on the music*] Here come the Nineties! [*Silence*] ... Fuck's sake ...

* [*The* **Woman** *holds up her hand – wait. She walks to the music player. The* **Woman** *puts her ear close to the sound system, listens. Suddenly the Nineties' soundscape bursts loudly into life, a mix of news and music*]

Em What the … ? [*Instead of posing,* **Em** *addresses the audience from the suitcase*] Don't worry ladies and gents. I'm gonna edit this down, this is the abridged version. Bottom line: Right to Buy went from strength to strength. Thanks to Blair, my parents are proud homeowners. These are their sounds. The sounds of my parents' youth.

* [*They listen to the soundscape. Meanwhile* **Em** *goes to the wall, takes down a few photos of her estate's residents: all different ages, all nationalities, all eating and playing together …*]

Woman [*inspecting the photos*] Marvellous! Utopia! Like a village hall!

Em [*remembering*] The residents made us snacks to take, isn't it?

* [**Em** *goes to switch off the music*]

Sarah [*digging around in the suitcase and brings out the homemade snacks*] … Kensal House was designed by this hard core Leftie.

Em [*to audience*] Word. Maxwell / Fry.

Woman Actually, *Elizabeth Denby* was the social reformer! *She* was the one who saw estates as villages … [*tucking into the snacks* **Sarah** *proffers with greedy appreciation*] … *She* had the vision for bettering the lives of urban poor, though she got no /credit!

Em [*to* **Woman**] Madam those snacks were for / everyone?

Woman [*wrestling to keep the snacks as* **Em** *tries to take them*] … Excuse me, excuse me?! … [*relinquishing the snacks with a hiccup*]

Em [*as the* **Woman** *noisily licks her fingers*] We got fed up calling the TMO, the council's 'tenants /management'

Sarah … begging them to fix stuff, begging them to just do their /job.

Em The/ landlord

Sarah [*to the audience*] 'Arm's length.'

Em So we fixed the hall up ourselves.

Woman [*burping loudly*] … Well, I feel *much better*! …

* [*The* **Woman** *turns to the sound system, cups her hand to her ear – over to you?* Under Pressure *by David Bowie kicks in. The* **Woman** *hums to the music as* **Sarah** *strains unsuccessfully to free her hand. When* **Em** *makes to turn the music off, the* **Woman** *grabs her hand also.* **Em** *and* **Sarah** *share a look – now what?*]

Woman I'm sorry – holding hands … is that not cool?

* [**Em** *and* **Sarah** *try to remove their hands as the music plays on. But the* **Woman**'s *grip is surprisingly firm*]

Woman I've never been cool, in fact, even as a child or teenager… [**Em** *and* **Sarah** *share a look*] Ah, I'm so immutable… Like a function… x = x=x=x… How I *didn't* change, *that's* what surprised! … My stubborn uncoolness as a baby playing eternal, the melody of my life! … [*Addresses the audience, conspiratorial*] … To be cool, you have not to care, or at least to act like you don't. And I do care. That much is obvious. Oh, it's unseemly! I *insist*! I admit it, you really do have to watch out for me!

Sarah [*still wrestling to break free*] Um… excuse me Madam?

Em Madam!

Woman Oh how I love to be told off! Told off by *people*. [*enjoying herself, to the audience*] We are our own church, aren't we? All each other's / saviours?

Em [*to* **Sarah**] Fucking God / botherer.

Woman Oh no, it's people I love! *People!* … [*amused*] Though I don't mind the devil, hot little fellow, bucking at the system … Where was / I?

Sarah Could you let go of our hands now, please?

Woman [*oblivious*] Oh yes! How I love *being seen!* ... [*To* **Em**] you were quite right, dear ... a trip here, a slip there, and *wump!* ... Yes, you got my number ... *Eyes on me* ... Wonderful!

Em [*to the audience*] I knew she faked that / fall?!

Woman And I'm a flirt too! I admit it! A terrible flirt! [*To* **Em** *and* **Sarah**] Flirting is knowing, flirting is glue; the glue of society, the sticky, delicious glue... [**Em** *catches her eye – with naked disgust*] ... I know what you think ... [**Em** *and* **Sarah** *continue wrestling to break free*] You think love is weak. You think *community* is weak; a soft option, for those who've failed, who've lost the big greedy race. For the stupid, for failures. Well, I disagree.

Em Look, you are *squashing our fingers?!*

Woman Love is political! Love is knowledge! The answer to indifference, the solution to fear! ... [*She approaches the audience*] Love is the dance, the fight that locks and unites, love is the wonderful war! Love is what raises us up, the battle worth fighting, love is the only thing that brings real change!

* [*Unwittingly, the* **Woman** *has released* **Em** *and* **Sarah** *and twirls out into the audience.* **Sarah** *watches the* **Woman***, beguiled despite herself.* **Em** *wrings out her sore hands*]

Woman Oh I know love's annoying [*to* **Em**] Like you, dear ... [*To* **Sarah**] Isn't your friend annoying? ... [*Chubbing* **Em***'s cheek*] We annoying people *love* to piss off! ... [*Picking out a couple from the audience*] You're pissed off, she's annoying? [*Picking out another couple*] You're grumpy, she's 'joy! joy! joy!'? [*Realising her mistake*] No no no *you* look after *him, he's* the one that keeps messing up! *He's* the child, it's *you* that's really lived! [*Giving the thumbs up*] Ah it takes both, yes it works both ways, men can be women, women men, I'm very 'gender fluid', very modern ... [*Twirling through the audience, picking*

Woman (*cont.*) *couples out*] You're 'excitable puppy', you're weary with experience, she's insanely fearless, he's secretly got the fear [*Twirling faster towards* **Em** *and* **Sarah**] I'm 'lucky, lucky, lucky' and you, *you* …

* [*The* **Woman**'s *twirling brings her to a halt, open armed, in front of* **Sarah**]

Woman … have suffered?

* [*The music flicks off with a crackle. Somehow, spell is broken.* **Sarah** *recoils*]

Woman I see.

* [*The* **Woman**'s *arms fall to her side*] Goodbye then, dear.

Sarah …You're leaving?

Woman I'm extremely late, I'm fantastically in demand, there's somewhere I really must be.

Em [*wiggling her fingers in a mocking little wave*] Shame.

Woman [*slowly mounting anger*] You can't wait to get rid of me, can you? … [**Em** *smirks*] … You inauthentic, self-centred little twerp! And to think, I've been wasting my *experience* on you? You just kick out *knowledge* like some bag of old bones! You've no sense of fellowship, / *no* …

Em Is you quoting the bible?

Woman I'm quoting *me*? [*To the audience*] I've been trying to educate this young fool because usually, I'm *good* at this, the way others might be good a sport, or sex! Because helping others makes me happy! Because I'm good at being happy!

Em [*to audience, sarcastic*] *Well* 'happy'? … [*To* **Woman**] You leavin' or what?

Woman [*deflated*] … Actually, I'm feeling rather out of sorts … [*To* **Sarah**] Would it be alright if I stayed a little longer?

Sarah Of course.

* [**Em** *palms her forehead in frustration. Sudden brainwave.* **Sarah** *takes* **Em** *aside*]

Em [*conspiratorial*] Sa, what if she's homeless?

Sarah Fuck off. She's like, an academic?

Em No Sa, think about it? She's crazy, she wears all her clothes at once, and she's gotta drink problem. Plus she's a drugs fiend. And lonely, she said it herself. I bet she ain't got a single mate she can stay with. We can't let her stay, we'll never get rid of / her.

Woman What are you girls whispering about? …

* [*Awkward silence*]

Em [*to* **Woman**] Listen, I know you said you never lie and that, but when you said you had loads of mates … you weren't telling porkie pies, was you?

Woman I said I was in demand … all my friends are dead …

Sarah … I'm truly sorry to hear that … is there anything we can do to help?

Woman … perhaps I could quickly smoke that 'joint'?

* [**Em** *gestures wildly at the clock, but* **Sarah** *ignores her*]

Woman I'm afraid your friend rather gets on my nerves.

Sarah [*seeking out the joint*] Tell me about it.

* [**Em** *stomps off to sit with the audience*]

Woman A quick puff is just what I need … take the edge off existence.

Sarah [*passes her the joint*] It's not real.

Woman I didn't imagine there'd be any *marijuana* in it … [*Lighting up*] D'you know though, going through the motions can almost gets me high? … [*Inhaling*] It's the memories, I think… powerful things, quite trippy sometimes … ever noticed that?

Sarah [*as the* **Woman** *lights up*] I'll just open the window.

* [**Sarah** *walks to the window, tries and fails to remove the blackout material in order to open it. The joint calms the* **Woman**]

Woman Typical…

Sarah [*still trying to open the window*] What?

Woman [*inhaling*] … our trapped freedoms?

Sarah [*still trying, increasingly frustrated*] It's just a window … it's just a bit stuck…

Woman [*inhaling*] It's symbolic.

Sarah [*still trying, increasingly frustrated*] I don't know about / that.

Woman [*calm, still smoking*] You don't know that beneath it all, we're all raging? … You don't see the simmering, spreading, raging rage? … [*Inhaling*] I think you /do …

Sarah [*turning away from the window*] Could you just stop talking for a minute?

* [*The* **Woman** *passes* **Sarah** *the joint*]

Woman D'you mind if I say something?

Sarah Will it take long?

Woman [*watching* **Sarah** *smoke*] … It's not gone unnoticed. The battle. The battle you're fighting with your brain.

Sarah Look, I'm not really up for chatting right now. I'd love to call it a day on the world's worst play but my mate would never let me hear the fucking end of it.

Woman I'm almost finished … [**Sarah** *bristles*] … I see how your mind torments you. And I'm sorry.

Sarah Please shut up.

Woman I've seen it before, you see … In my friends … My best friends.

Sarah Sorry?

Woman And I always say: if you tell me … I'm facing fear, utter fear … Then I'll feel … of course … I'll feel … You're very brave.

Sarah You've got me confused with someone else.

Woman I see. I do see.

Sarah [*more irritated*] *What* do you 'see'?

Woman Inside you … Some people call it your soul … I call it your ghost? …

* [**Sarah** *stubs out the 'spliff' and stands, tense*]

Em Sa, she didn't mean that kind of ghost?

Sarah Leave me alone. Both of you. Please.

Em Babe …

Sarah [*impersonating, high-pitched*] 'Babe' 'babe'.

Em Sa, if this is about…

Sarah You promised! You said we wouldn't talk about that here?

Em Sa, but I never said it, I never /said?

Sarah You / *said*

Em It's called The Burning Tower? It's / *about*

Sarah Shut up! Shut up!

* [**Sarah** *puts her hands over her ears*]

Sarah [*rapping, gently at first but with growing passion*]
  Goddam, I'm almost there
  My heart's in my ears, I hear it, I swear
  Thump, thump – bang
  Man, I can't contain it!
  Watch me spit and crack and split
  Do you know what living is?
  Do you know what it is to hate or kiss?
  I remember, I can't delete my brain

If that's crazy then I'm utterly insane
Have you heard the smoke come crackle and hiss?
A million melting pieces
Burn divide inside
Anyone been on fire?
Anyone gotta mind?
Anyone ever died?

* [*A fire alarm goes off.* **Sarah** *walks to the window*]

Em [*to audience*] Don't worry, all these places have dodgy electrics. It's just a fault, it'll go off soon …

Woman Are you sure?

* [**Sarah** *resumes trying to open the window. As her desperation mounts, residents' recorded voices, including* **Tom**'s, *join the sounds of the fire alarm from all around*]

Resident [*recorded*] They say seventy-two died … But it must be hundreds.

Tom [*recorded*] It's wrong to care more for cash than people …

Council worker [*well-spoken, recorded*] We ring-fenced the sell-off to pay for the cladding.

Tom [*recorded*] Monopoly houses, empty … when people are homeless?

Resident [*recorded*] Twenty-four floors and all over floor four told to stay put? …

* [**Sarah** *turns from the window, takes off her jumper; beneath her vest, a scar between* **Sarah**'s *heart and collar bone is visible. She continues to talk over the voices, heard now on a loop*]

Sarah Is it hot in here? Can someone open the door?

Tom [*recorded*] The flames spread faster…

Em [*placating* **Sarah**] It's open, Sa.

Resident [*recorded*] The rich get richer …

Sarah Is there a fridge? Is the fridge overheating?

Tom [*recorded*] It's harder and harder for the poor …

Em Sa there's no fridge …

TMO worker [*recorded, well-spoken*] The costlier jobs get lower priority.

Tom [*recorded*] The rate the flames spread at increases over time …

* [*The recorded voices continue on a loop as* **Sarah** *walks out to address different audience*]

Sarah Has there been another surge? … Did you call the TMO? … Be careful, the windows are faulty! … Don't trip … Watch out for those wires, they're not boxed in! … Where will the engines park? … Remember, there's no fire doors! … Did you shut the door on the flames? … [*As* **Sarah**'s *panic grows,* **Em** *turns away; the* **Woman** *goes to* **Sarah**] … The smoke's getting bad now … it's bad, it's getting worse … it's got worse so quick … so fast, too fast … don't breathe it … don't breathe it … can't breathe … I can't breathe … can't breathe … I can't …

* [**Sarah** *moves towards the door. The* **Woman** *blocks her way.* **Sarah** *moves left. The* **Woman** *does the same.* **Sarah** *moves right as does the* **Woman**. *The* **Woman** *reaches out to* **Sarah**. **Sarah** *gets out a knife, threatens the* **Woman**. *The fire alarm and voices suddenly stop. Silence.* **Em** *turns, registers what's going on*]

Em Fuck fuck *fucking* fuck …

* [**Em** *stays rooted to the spot. The* **Woman** *calmly reaches out to the knife that's threatening her and takes it.* **Em** *clears her throat*]

Em [*to the audience*] Sorry 'bout that, folks … just a slight overreaction … blades come with the territory, unfortunately … part of estate life … protection…

Sarah [*incensed*] … Protection … '*Protection*'?! [*To the* **Woman**] Can I have my knife back please?

* [*The* **Woman** *meets her eye. The tension grows*]

Sarah [*shouting*] Give me back my fucking knife!

* [*The* **Woman** *slowly shakes her head. Beside herself,* **Sarah** *starts to pick her scar*]

Em Oh God … Sa … stop … don't pick at it …

* [**Sarah** *stares straight ahead, catatonic.* **Woman** *goes to the suitcase, brings out the first aid. Her movements an untheatrical and efficient*]

Em [*to the audience*] … she got that scar in the fire.

Woman Really? … [*Inspecting*] That doesn't look like a burn to me … [*To* **Em**] dear?

Em [*miserable*] I'm not supposed to talk about it.

* [**Woman** *uses antiseptic to clean the blood from* **Sarah**'*s body, though the wound remains*]

Em Sorry, Sa.

* [**Em** *holds out her arms.* **Sarah** *remains catatonic*]

Em Can't you just say it's OK?

* [**Em**'*s arms flump to her sides. The* **Woman** *crouches down, looks* **Sarah** *in the eye*]

Woman I know you can hear me … your friend is trying, you know … … Don't punish her?

* [**Sarah** *closes her eyes a moment, then opens them and sees the* **Woman** *staring right at her. Blinks despite herself.* **Em** *approaches*]

Woman [*to* **Em**] That poem you gave us about the Greeks was spot on, by the /way…

Em I wanted to rap it, but I'm too shit.

* [**Em** *blows her nose*]

Woman I liked your delivery. It felt right, / for

Em [*to* **Sarah**] It's OK; we won't say it … [*To* **Woman**] She
doesn't like us to say it.

Woman Say what?

Sarah … Grenfell.

* [**Em** *and the* **Woman** *look at* **Sarah**. **Sarah**'s *hand returns to
her scar*]

Sarah [*small voice*] It's ugly, isn't it…? I've made it worse,
haven't I?

Em [*kind*] No Sa, it's fine … it's fine.

Sarah Is it?

Em I just told you?

Sarah [*to* **Woman**] It won't ever be fine, will it?

Em But / Sa …

Woman [*to* **Em**, *offering her the notepad*] Would you give
these out for me, dear? One per person, they're all
numbered? For the campaign?

Em But…

Woman It would mean such a lot to me. And there's just
something I'd like to tell your friend.

Sarah Please, Em?

* [**Em** *obliges, ripping out the notes, distributing them to
audience as the* **Woman** *talks on*]

* [*The sounds of the space cut out, upping the tension*]

Woman [*to* **Sarah**, *confiding*] Someone I loved suffered very
deeply … 'depression,' 'anxiety' 'mental health,' such
weak words … But we both know … that kind of pain is
strong … it takes strength just to face it, not to give up …
It's terror, it's fear writ large … it's pain that feels like it'll
never fade … My loved one's anguish *burned* … Oh, it was
in her head; but it was also real, the suffering is always
real, d'you understand? … Hurt that made her angry and

Woman (*cont.*) so, so lonely, made her push everyone away … A kind of panic, endless … Like losing a child … searching, always searching … I'd almost forgotten … People banging on doors, waking each other up … Running through smoke, babes in arms … Brave, magnificent, ordinary people … told to stay in their flats but knowing, knowing not to … flames licking upwards, tenfold, magnified … I saw hell that night … you might not have seen me, but I saw you…

* [*The* **Woman** *reaches out towards* **Sarah**'s *scar.* **Sarah** *returns her gaze – is she mesmerised?*]

Woman [*to* **Sarah**] I'm on one side. You're on the other. But that doesn't matter, does it?

* [*Just as the* **Woman** *is about to touch* **Sarah**, **Em** *returns to give back the notebook. Letting go of* **Sarah**'s *hand, the* **Woman** *takes it*]

Sarah I'd like to carry on, if that's OK? I'd like to do modern day?

Woman Shall I stay? … [**Sarah** *nods*] … I'll be right here … [**Woman** *sits at* **Sarah**'s *feet*]

* [**Sarah** *opens her eyes and flinches at the audience's gaze*]

Woman Would it help if we closed our eyes?

* [**Sarah** *nods*]

Em Close your eyes please, thanks.

Sarah [*suddenly serious*] This is the sound of my youth.

[*The* **Woman** *gestures to the sound system, puts her hand to her ear*]

* [*It's Stormzy's* Blinded by Your Grace Part 2. *After the hymn like introduction,* **Em** *sings the first eight lines, psyching herself up. The verse continues on a loop as* **Em** *goes to sit with the audience*]

Sarah [*to audience*] My Gran took in Mum and me ... Her flat's opposite ... Opposite 'The Burning Tower' ... where we used to live ... [*Brief eye contact with* **Em**] ... What this show, what everything, is about ... Every day I look out the window ... I try not to look ... but the more I avoid it, the more it's there... ... however they dress it up, it's still a corpse, a skeleton ... windows gaping like eye sockets ... I'm looking, I can't stop looking, but no one's looking back? ...

* [*Clearing her throat,* **Em** *stands*]

Em It's people like you kept the death toll down. The point is, you're a hero.

Sarah That's a nice thing to say.

Em [*to the audience*] This girl went back through the flames, saved her Mum, dragged her out. When she was too scared to move.

Sarah Right. But somehow ... I'm still looking?

Em No no no, but Sa ... you found your Mum?

Sarah What if she didn't want to be found?

* [*Music continues*]

Sarah I'm just being honest, Em; no one wants us. My Gran's got enough problems without us puking our nightmares all over her couch. She's been worried sick ... worried about where she'll live ...

Em That's why the show? To stop places like Silchester being torn down? To save your flat?

Sarah It's not our flat though is it? ... Emma, do you really have to make me say it? We own *nothing* ... *We're not like you?* ... [*Ignoring* **Em** *'s gesture of protest*] ... You think 'cos *you* love your estate, *we're* protected? You think it *surrounds us all* ... You think we can *stop them tearing it down?* ... Yes the show matters ... these buildings matter... their history matters ...but 'welfare', *real welfare?* ... Emma it's gone...

Sarah (*cont.*) it's long, long gone? … [*To* **Woman**] and it's like what they're bulldozing *now*… is what's inside, the 'ghost,' the thing you called 'soul'? … like kindness is crumbling… years' worth of caring, all turning to dust … [**Em** *takes this in*] … Yeah you live round the corner but Emma, your flat is a million miles away! … you don't shiver at breakfast 'cause you can't afford heat *and* bread … You don't hear the voices your Mum hears, or *her* Mum, telling you you're *crap, useless* … or the voices of your friends, *screaming* to be saved … … your hands don't *shake,* you don't struggle to b*reathe,* you don't get so scared you *can't move* or talk … You don't sit at the bottom, looking up … watching how money makes money, … and floats, and floats, and never falls?

Em [*switching the music off*] It's OK, Sa… Your Gran'd never kick you out…

Sarah Emma, my Gran's going back to Jamaica…

Em Wait… what?

Sarah You know how stressed she's been … you know how old she is, you watch the news…

Em … 'Windrush'?

Sarah Sorry, is that not what this show is / about?

Em But … didn't they…

Sarah It's too late…

Em No no no but, didn't /they

Sarah 'They'? *They* don't get panic attacks! Or lawyers' bills! Or 'regeneration' letters that keep them up fretting all night! They don't feel unsafe and *unwelcome* where they've lived half their lives! Everyone has a limit, Em! And *some* pride! They told her to leave, she's leaving!

Em But … where'll you live?

Sarah I don't know, Emma. You tell me.

* [*The sounds of the space fade out to encourage a new intimacy*]

Sarah That's not what I meant to say … I'm not a whinger … What I wanted to say was … for all their sympathy, people hate on Grenfell … 'Grenfell the death trap' – and it was, they're right: but … it was our home? …

* [*Smiles despite herself, remembering*]

Sarah The residents' room? Best place in the tower! I mean yeah there was not much spent on it, like here – but we loved it! Loved that no one would *dream* of putting it on Instagram! Loved its total shitness! … [*To* **Woman**] And yeah, life *was* tough, people got hurt … but it was ours?

Woman Yes. We hear you.

Sarah [*to the* **Woman**] Do you? … Tom said energy lives forever … 'the law of physics' … I reckon he's wrong … whoever made that stupid rule never lost someone, never cried themselves sick, wanting what's gone … the laughter, the shit that made all the awful shit bearable? You feel it, like an ache, a shadow, a lost leg …

Woman and yet, it's *nowhere* …

Sarah vanished …

Woman how? …

Sarah why? …

Woman where?

* [*Pause.* **Sarah**'s *surprised*]

Sarah [*to* **Woman**] … you really do get it, don't you?

Woman Yes.

Sarah You don't give a shit I'm not posh like you … … you really do respect me? … Do you like, want to be my *friend*?

Woman Yes. I do.

Sarah [*incredulous*] Fuck off.

* [*Pause*]

Woman … It is OK, you know … to / ask…

Sarah Not my style.

Woman No. You shouldn't have to. And unfortunately, I have nothing, financially, to offer. But if there's something else you need, please tell me. I promise I'll listen.

Sarah I need my knife?

* [*The* **Woman** *gets out the knife. Gives it to* **Sarah**]

Em What the hell d'you think you're doing?

Woman I'm returning her property? She said she needed it?

Em You know what she'll do with that, don't you?

Woman 'Protection'? 'Gangs', I think you said? … [**Em** *bristles*] … Or something else, perhaps? Whatever it is, I don't imagine you prefer that she do it in secret…

Em Well tell the lady! Tell her what you do! See if she 'gets it'?!

Sarah [*to the* **Woman**] …it makes me feel better. Or it used to. Now it doesn't work so well … I have to cut deeper, I /have

Em Give me that blade right now!

* [**Sarah** *contemplates the knife*]

Em Sa this is killing me … [*to* **Woman**] it's killing me for years …, and now, *now*, since…

Sarah Grenfell?

Woman [*to* **Sarah**] Why do you cut yourself, dear?

* [**Sarah** *traces the knife's blade with her finger*]

Sarah [*to* **Em**] You don't need to worry … I just need to know it's there … [*To* **Woman**] a last resort thing … … 'mental', right?

Woman I think you're the sanest person I've met.

Sarah For real?

* [**Sarah** *puts the knife away*]

Sarah [*calm, to the audience*] I'm not here to blame anyone. But the truth is I'm not fine. [*Silence*] Not cause I'm stupid or lazy or deserve it, but cause in my shoes, you wouldn't be fine either. Cause if you're poor *now*, you stay that way. That's not what we *learned*, from *research*, pre-war, post-war, Fifties, Sixties, Seventies; this is *now* – and it's never, *never* been worse. Yeah some people have cheap holidays, Sky subscriptions – but people like us? The people on minimum wage? The people with sickness, not 'cool' sick, *really* too sick to work? The people this country tells to be '*grateful*'? The people England judges and watches and never helps? … [*To* **Woman**] … I need help! I need your help! There, I said it! …

Em But Sa, /I …

Sarah Emma, you don't. You don't help at all. Because Emma, Grenfell wasn't a movie, a boast, a badge of honour, some cool street cred. And actually, you weren't there. If you were, you'd get why I want to forget.

Em But Sa, they can't just get away with it?

Sarah Who? Who exactly are you talking about, Emma? *What* are you talking about?

Em Wait … what?

Sarah The fireman we interviewed, that big guy that kept seeing flames? … He begged for ladders, he had to borrow to stay in budget … Or that caretaker, the man with five kids, blubbing like a baby? … He fixed what he could, but he had to work six estates, … Even the TMO, they're not all 'fat cats', they miss their targets, they lose

Sarah (*cont.*) their jobs – and even if they are, even if they're rolling in it … I'll bet you none of them can sleep any more than I can … The hate doesn't help, Ems …

Em But Sa, you deserve better. Man, you're /a…

Sarah There weren't any 'heroes'. There was nothing but trapped people, burning flesh and pain. And I tell you what, most of us 'heroes'? We're still trapped … children breaking through boarding, digging up rubble, looking for friends cause no one's man enough to tell them that 'missing'? … Missing means *dead*. … Trapped because people pretend … block their ears … leave us burning inside.

Em Sa babe, blud, blud man listen … I real you, Sa

Sarah You 'real' me? …

* [**Sarah** *bursts out laughing*]

Sarah Emma, it's 'I *feel* you'! Oh my God, Emma, you're such a *fake?*

* [**Em**'s *shame is disarming – she tries to pull herself together*]

Em [*the music volume gradually increasing*] But Sarah, I do 'feel' you … *I feel you* … I feel you like if you're hurting, I hurt, you know? … and you're right, I *don't* know Grenfell … I never lived there, my estate's different, my flat, my life, it's different, you're right … but I do know *you?* … I'm not faking that, Sa; I've known you forever … I know you shouldn't *have to always* be brave … you shouldn't have to feel *scared shitless*, and come like you're *not* … you shouldn't have to go through all that on your own … I feel you 'cos you're a part of me … I feel you cause, to *me* … you've always been home?

* [**Sarah**'s *at a loss, wrong-footed*]

Sarah [*embarrassed*] Laters, Em … There's a time and a place … I am done people staring at me.

Em [*as* **Sarah** *makes to leave*] But Sa you can't go, *you* love me! … I *know* you love me … 'cos I love you? … [**Sarah** *halts*] … I feel it! I feel it! I know you feel it too! It's like Tom said, magnets and, *and* … … magnetic force … … stuck together … locked together … the force, the same force…

Sarah God Emma, getta girlfriend?

Em No no no but, fuck's sake! Yeah if you was a bloke then I'd probably fancy you but you're not so I don't! What's it matter? Am I s'posed to feel *bad*? Sure, be frightened of fridges and closed windows, smoke, darkness, fine – but *me*? You're fucking afraid of *me*?! …

* [*Music fades out*]

Em … You are so fucking annoying …

Sarah *I'm* annoying?

Em Fuck yeah! … Knowing you back to front, knowing when you're fronting it out? Knowing how pig-headed you are, how you won't say when you're pissing your pants? [*Growing more emotional,* **Em** *frets*] Knowing you won't let me in, even when you need it, 'cos you're a stubborn bitch, and you're the one that's always gotta be strong … I *get* you, you stupid cow … I *know* you … I'd never *judge* you … *I love you* … … I'm your *friend*?

* [*Slowly,* **Sarah** *approaches.* **Em** *succumbs to her emotions*]

Sarah [*gentle*] Oh Ems…

* [**Em** *sniffs. After a moment,* **Sarah** *puts an arm around her friend*]

Em I've fucked everything up, haven't I?

Sarah [*affectionate*] No change there then?

Em Em is for muppet … Em is for middle class moron …

Sarah [*shy*] … I'd like to be middle class. I'd like to be like you.

Em [*surprised*] … I'd like to be like you.

[*Pause*]

Sarah Sometimes though Em, could you may be … pipe down … and listen?

Em … I have listened?

* [**Sarah** *looks at* **Em** *questioningly*]

Em You and your Mum come stay with us.

* [*The lights suddenly flick on.* **Em** *and* **Sarah** *look around, dazed*]

Sarah It wasn't the cladding or fridge that killed my friends, it was being ignored.

* [*The tension builds.* **Em** *moves towards* **Sarah**, *her arms outstretched*]

Em I hear you… …stay with us?

* [*But* **Sarah** *still holds back. The* **Woman** *steps into* **Em***'s arms and hugs her. Slowly, they release each other*]

Em [*to the* **Woman**] Sorry, madam. Sorry for calling you an old witch.

Woman Sorry for calling you inauthentic. You're not in the slightest inauthentic.

Em What's *not* inauthentic?

Woman It means you're real … a real person … [*tenderly stroking* **Em***'s cheek*] It means you're alive.

* [**Em** *smiles. The* **Woman** *smiles back*]

Em Thank you. For everything.

* [*The* **Woman** *bows to* **Em**. *Then she bows to* **Sarah**. *Then to everyone. If anyone starts to clap, she holds up a hand to stop them. For a moment, the* **Woman***'s emotions get the better of her.* **Sarah** *puts an arm around her*]

Woman Oh I'm not sad. I've had a wonderful time. I'm happy. [*Bittersweet*] *Happy.*

* [*The* **Woman** *pulls herself together with a little laugh, stands a little taller. As she lets her hair down, we glimpse the girl deep in her heart*]

Woman [*taking* **Em** *and* **Sarah**'s *hands, kissing* **Sarah**'s *cheek*] My beautiful girls … [*Kissing* **Em**'s *cheek*] You girls are my heart … green hearts growing … love … out of ash. [*The* **Woman** *holds the girls' eyes, directs them to follow hers towards the Grenfell heart*] … Your roots are strong … [*Finding her strength*] … You'll burst through the concrete … You'll survive, of course you will … [*To the audience*] You are all me. We are all each other … I can be dignified now … I can go.

* [*Off, there's a single knock at the door.* **Em**, **Sarah** *and the* **Woman** *look round*]

Em The fucking council … We're out of time.

Woman [*suddenly business-like*] Leave this to me. [*The* **Woman** *starts to make for the door*]

Sarah Wait!

* [*The* **Woman** *halts.* **Sarah** *approaches the* **Woman**, *but finds herself at a loss as what to say.* **Sarah** *takes out the knife, considers it. As the silence grows, so does* **Em**'s *agitation*]

Sarah I can do this.

* [**Sarah** *gives the* **Woman** *the knife*]

Em [*to herself*] Oh thank God, thank you … thank you …

* [*Another knock.* **Woman** *resumes walking*]

Sarah … You will come back? [*The* **Woman** *is oddly pleased by this. She smiles*]

Woman I don't generally just disappear …

* [*Several knocks this time. The* **Woman**'s *footsteps as she walks now are increasingly graceful, youthful and elegant*]

Woman [*over her shoulder*] Goodbye, my beloved campaigners! Don't forget my dear list!

        * [*Exit the* **Woman**, *who disappears via the exit off*

Em Now what?

Sarah That list … it was numbered, wasn't it?

Em Wait … what?

Sarah One… Who had one…? [*Pointing to the audience member with 'one'*] … That was you?

Audience 'Having mates nearby.'

Sarah Two?

Audience 'Something to build on.'

Sarah Three?

Audience 'Somewhere to feel safe.'

Sarah Four?

Audience 'People to party with.'

Sarah Five?

Audience 'Shared spaces.'

Sarah Six?

Audience 'Places for the children to play.'

Sarah Seven?

Audience 'Someone to watch out for you.'

Sarah Eight?

Audience 'Someone you never need to ask.'

Sarah Nine?

Audience 'Who listens, when no one else will.'

Sarah Ten?

Audience Who never slags you off to anyone but you.'

Sarah Eleven?

Audience 'Who makes you better.'

Sarah Twelve?

Audience 'Someone with a sixth sense for your bullshit.'

Sarah Thirteen?

Audience 'Who always, always believes in you.'

Sarah Fourteen?

Audience 'Who knows you so well, it really gets on your tits.'

Sarah Fifteen?

Audience 'Who's there, wherever you are.'

* [*Silence.* **Em** *looks up from the* **Woman***'s notebook*]

Em [*flicking through the pages to show* **Sarah**] 'Who'd protect you, even if you couldn't see me' … 'Who'd take your knife, to stop you hurting yourself … 'Who'd give you light, if the dark made you scared … 'Who'd welcome you, if you were homeless.'

* [*A bell chimes.* **Sarah** *rushes to hug* **Em**. *We hear a news recording of the names of those who died in Grenfell.* **Em** *and* **Sarah** *sit together with the audience as they listen*]

Em … those are the names of the people who died in Grenfell … Grenfell's survivors have not been rehoused. More than 10,000 people sleep rough or in unsafe housing every year. 200,000 UK buildings are permanently empty. More than a hundred London estates are due to be torn down …

Sarah [*standing*] thank you everyone for coming, for joining our mailing list. Thank you for helping with our list of why social housing matters, it means a lot to us … Do have munch if you're staying to check out our

Sarah (*cont.*) exhibition. And do take a handout when you go … … It's great to have shared our learning, our history. [*Taking* **Em***'s hand, leading her to the centre of the space*] … Ready?

* [*Before* **Em** *and* **Sarah** *can bow, the sounds of demolition grow gradually from all around; bulldozers, drills, crumbling buildings. As the sounds get louder,* **Sarah** *raises their hands higher and, from her position in the middle, looks defiantly ahead*]

[*Blackout*

[*Exit* **Em** *and* **Sarah**

* [*When the lights come up,* **Em** *and* **Sarah** *have gone. Post-show music kicks in with the lights:* You've Got The Love *as covered by Florence and the Machine*]

Ivy

by

Helena Thompson

Cast

Ivy   Leda Hodgson
Chloe/Boss   Charlotte Salkind

Crew

Writer   Helena Thompson
Director   Mel Cook
Producer   Shan Rixon
Production Designer   Emily Megson
Production Manager   Federico Angelini
Sound Designer   Jordan Mallory-Skinner
Lighting Designer/Technical Director   Greg Jordan
Assistant Director/Stage Manager   Connie Treves

Thanks

Ivy was commissioned by BBC Radio 4 as *The Burning Times,* and was originally directed and produced for radio by Boz Temple Morris.

Ivy was first produced as a promenade production by S.P.I.D. with Southwark Playhouse. *Ivy* is dedicated to all my family – especially cousin Tom.

Set

The action takes place one evening in a squat. It has a door leading off to the rest of the building. The space has been partially taken over by evergreens; mostly vines like ivy, along with some flowering weeds which are also in vases. There is a functioning kettle, teapot, table, and radio.

Sound

In the course of the play the soundscape morphs from naturalism into something more heightened. The sounds seeping in from outside start off commonplace enough, but gradually the way the sounds start to distort hints at something more supernatural.

Time

The play is told in one act with no scene breaks or intervals and lasts about sixty minutes.

Note

/ denotes the point where the next speaker interrupts.

Characters

Ivy an articulate, elderly woman – seems vulnerable and uptight but is actually self-assured and uninhibited with a wry sense of humour.

Chloe is a teenage girl with a London accent – seems tough and bolshie but is actually sensitive and keen to please, with an idealistic nature.

Boss the leader of a teenage gang (played by the same actress who plays **Chloe**). She is heard mainly as an offstage recording, appearing only at the end.

Act One

The playing-in music is a strange tune, evocative of nature and growth. **Chloe** *is searching the squat. She finds a tin, opens it – it's empty.*

Enter **Ivy**, *emerging from hiding*

Ivy Get out.

Chloe Where's your money?

Ivy I've got nothing.

Chloe Five, four.

Ivy I swear I don't.

Chloe Two.

Ivy Please.

Chloe Last chance. [**Chloe**'s *phone beeps*] You're out of time. [**Chloe** *sets to ransacking the place*]

Ivy … please don't …

[*A bee starts buzzing. Then another*]

Chloe Urgh.

Ivy This is my home.

Chloe Insects. Grim.

Ivy Careful.

Chloe You want pest control.

Ivy Late season pollinators.

Chloe The fuck? [**Chloe** *continues ransacking*] Plants all over the shop. Rank.

Ivy Hedera. It creeps through the ceiling.

Chloe What the …

Ivy It's been creeping for years

Chloe Like you.

Ivy I asked you to leave.

Chloe Where's ya money?

Ivy Money?

Chloe I know you're lying. I can smell it.

Ivy With a nose full of snot?

Chloe [*sneezing*] Fuckin' hell …

Ivy Excuse me?

Chloe Whatta shithole! [*Something can be heard scuttling off. And another. And another*] Nice flatmates …

Ivy Rats can breed quickly.

Chloe A witch like you must be in her element.

Ivy You don't believe that.

[*Offstage there's a bang somewhere*]

Chloe Fuck me!

Ivy Perhaps they've started.

Chloe Right. Hand it over.

Ivy … All I have is flowers.

Chloe That's it.

Ivy There's plenty in the vase. You could sell them.

Chloe Yeah? [**Chloe** *threatens to yank some plants up by the roots*] You're freakin' out now, ain't cha?

Ivy Just you try it.

[*Viciously,* **Chloe** *yanks. Insects buzz in retaliation*]

Chloe Fucking bug bit me!

Ivy Leave my plants alone.

[*More banging of possible building work*]

Ivy Help! Help!

Chloe [*laughing*] 'Help! Help!'

Ivy Somebody, help me!

Chloe It's time you faced facts. You're an ole tramp, in some ole dump, an' no one wants you. No one gives a fuck about you an' your poxy plants. [*Hitting them, then sucking her finger*] Spiky fuckers.

Ivy [*gathers flowers from the vase*] Take this lot.

Chloe You must be shrooming.

Ivy Take them and go.

Chloe *Where is it?* [**Chloe** *starts to strangle* **Ivy**]

Ivy Let go of me, you –

Chloe Now don't you swear. It's disgusting when old people swear.

Ivy Sod off.

Chloe You are proper gettin' on my tits. [**Chloe** *tightens her grip*] A few hundred. At least. Come on now.

Ivy Not so tight.

Chloe I promised them.

Ivy Who?

Chloe My mates.

Ivy 'Mates'?

Chloe I have to. I have to deliver.

Ivy Why.

Chloe I'm chief, ain't I? I'm leader. I'm top dog.

[*Pause*]

Boss [*offstage recording*] Oi, bitch!

Chloe Christ's sake!

Boss [*offstage recording*] Bitch! … Oi, bitch! Get a move on, den!

Chloe Shit, shit …

Boss [*offstage recording*] We ain't got all day!

[*Rowdiness from offstage*]

Chloe [*starting to panic she grabs* **Ivy**'*s hands*] I'll bend your fingers back.

Boss [*offstage recording*] Just do it!

Ivy No … stop.

Boss [*offstage recording*] Do it!

Chloe Come on …

Ivy Not my hands … I need my hands

Chloe Come on, green fingers …

Boss [*offstage recording*] Do it!

Chloe Come on!!

Boss [*offstage recording*] Bitch! Bitch! Bitch!

[*Suddenly* **Chloe** *faints.* **Ivy** *looks at her. At a leisurely pace, she ambles and pours a cup of her tea*]

Ivy Hello … ? [**Chloe** *groans*] Can you hear me?

Chloe Eh?

Ivy You've had a bit of a turn …

Chloe What?

Ivy Your friends have gone now.

Chloe Oh … [*rallying herself.* **Ivy** *sets the cup down*] What's that?

Ivy Just tea.

Chloe Looks like rotting leaves.

Ivy You may not like it.

Chloe I'll be the judge o'that. [**Chloe** *sips*] Not bad. Bitter. But sweet. [**Chloe** *sips more*] You look like I'm drinkin' baby's blood!

Ivy No.

Chloe It's quite moreish – in a rank kind of way … My mates was right, you is medieval.

Ivy Hardly.

Chloe One dem ole birds; strapped to stool, float or sink, innit!

Ivy You should leave. It's not safe.

Chloe You still here, ain't cha?

Ivy Developers don't scare me. Screw them and their plans. I know my rights.

Chloe You wanna stay? [**Chloe** *tries to get up, sways*]

Ivy Steady.

Chloe [*laughing at herself*] Woah … jus' get me bearings.

Ivy You're not going anywhere

Chloe [*sitting down*] You might be right. Hey, that's funny that is … it's like, I'm your hostage! … Innit! Innit, right? [**Chloe** *belches*] Well excuse me! [**Chloe** *giggles and finally calms down*] … Is it plants, den? It plants wha' I drank?

Ivy Yes.

Chloe I drank ya potion?

Ivy Well.

Chloe You've put me under a spell … You know what you're doing, don't you?

Ivy My plants know what they're doing.

Chloe Wha' they do, den?

Ivy They can calm you down, or wake you up.

Chloe You've bewitched me. I knew you was a witch!

Ivy No.

Chloe Really?

Ivy No.

Chloe Really really?

Ivy No.

Chloe Really really really?

Ivy No. These weeds haven't done anything, your body's just recovering. You obviously had some kind of attack.

Chloe Shut it, yeah?

[**Ivy** *continues tidying*]

Chloe What are you doin'?

Ivy Everything … in its … place

Chloe Not gettin' very far, are ya? Don't worry, I won't try anything. I get these panic wotsits, if you must know. That thing just now. When I … (collapsed)

Ivy I see.

Chloe … Come like I'm gonna peg it.

Ivy Oh?

Chloe Ain't no pussy. Bear Grylls'd freak, d'you get me?

Ivy Right.

Chloe It's like … when you tink somefing bad's comin' … really bad … an ain't notin' you can do.

Ivy What's your doctor say?

Chloe Ain't got a doctor.

Ivy A walk-in?

Chloe Why'd I go there?

Ivy Valium.

Chloe You spazz out too?

Ivy Sometimes. Yes.

Chloe You dark horse. [**Chloe** *laughs*] That tea's a slow burner. I feel quite good on it now. Better than hash!

Ivy I think so.

Chloe Yeah right, like you'd know.

Ivy I might.

Chloe Yeah?

Ivy I couldn't afford it now.

Chloe Tell me about it … you have got enough, haven't you?

Ivy What?

Chloe Enough to get by.

Ivy Oh yes. I'm a survivor.

Chloe Wow. You crack me up.

Ivy What?

Chloe 'I'm a survivor.' What are you like?

Ivy Have you finished?

[**Chloe** *nods.* **Ivy** *takes the cup*]

Chloe What I drink, then?

Ivy This and that. Bit of heliotrope, some Valerian. Those two don't mind flowering this time of year. I added some wormwood too – always nice and potent, and sturdy, good for wreaths in the festive season.

Chloe Your tea's well trippy, that's what I reckon.

Ivy It can make you feel odd – if you're not yourself.

Chloe People pay to get high.

Ivy Do they?

Chloe Course.

Ivy Oh.

Chloe You better show me how to make it. Go on.

Ivy … OK. [**Ivy** *selects some plants from the jars*] Always keep your different plants separate.

Chloe Where do plants come from, then?

Ivy What's important is their leaves.

Chloe Wow … dis is *complex.*

Ivy We're using leaves and also roots. They come from trees or shrubs.

Chloe Trees, yeah.

Ivy [*chopping the plants*] What shall we put in first?

Chloe … A tree!

Ivy We don't have any trees in here. What about the Valerian?

Chloe Val-er-i-an.

Ivy Am I boring you?

Chloe Nah man, I'm intest, intest – in-ter-est-ed. [**Chloe** *giggles, drowsy*] You're very clever, you know. Has anyone ever told you that? I don't think I've ever met anyone as clever as you. I mean … f'real. [*A bee buzzes*] There's something about your voice. The things you say ... I know dem true. [**Chloe** *yawns*] Yer words, yer sentences ... like songs. Really gets inside yer head ... d'you get me? [**Chloe**'s *phone beeps with a text message. She's too blissed out to notice at first. Then she looks at it*] Code black. Three minutes. [**Chloe** *pulls herself together*] You got any coffee?

Ivy Oh ... I'll have to see.

Chloe Everyone got coffee, fam.

Ivy Will this do? It's passed its sell-by.

Chloe Instant don't go off.

[**Ivy** *switches on the kettle.* **Chloe** *starts pacing*]

Chloe I really need a pick me up, you get me?

Ivy Could you stop pacing please? You look rather green.

Chloe Do I? Stupid really. Boss, right, she acts tough.

Ivy I thought you were Boss?

Chloe *Boss.*

Ivy I see.

[*Pause*]

Chloe Everyone knows I'm in charge. Silly innit, I always like humour her. Shouldn't really.

Ivy Not if you're 'top dog.'

Chloe Are you takin' the piss?

[*Pause*]

Ivy So this is about your friends?

Chloe Ting is, you might ... meet them.

Ivy Well that's hardly a problem. I've been 'meeting them' for years.

Chloe It is a problem, innit.

Ivy Really?

Chloe Can I tell you something?

Ivy If you stop jumping round like a flea.

[**Chloe** *stops*]

Chloe I didn't want to come here, right?

Ivy Oh?

Chloe It took me ages to come in the door … And then when I saw you … all dried up … all lookin' like you's gonna die or some shit … I thought I was gonna bottle …

Ivy I don't follow.

Chloe I thought that buzzing bee was in my head … I thought my brain would explode …

Ivy How unusual.

Chloe Not for me … I need dat cash, you get me? … Boss needs it … It were a dare, right?

Ivy A dare. Sounds rather childish …

Chloe You don't get it. Pussy out, I'm done for, right?

Ivy And?

Chloe I ain't Boss! I'm *Bitch*! Bitches gets dared! Bitches get done! I'm fucked! [*Pause*] I shouldn't of come here. What shall I do?

Ivy I think it's about time you took charge.

Chloe You wha'? [**Chloe** *starts pacing again*] This ain't no game, you know … Boss is broke, her lot's fearless … Some dem huge – why you tink dem call me bitch?

Ivy It's got nothing to do with that.

Chloe She's fucking mental. *Loves* callin' de shots. She should fucking lay off.

Ivy If she knows what's good for her …

Chloe Wha'? [**Ivy** *says nothing*] I wish somefing bad would get her, fuck's sake.

Ivy Of course.

Chloe F'real! I wish something really bad would knock that smug grin off her face. Give us all a break.

Ivy Right.

Chloe … You look shocked. [*The kettle boils*] You think I'm bein' harsh …

Ivy What is it that you're trying to tell me?

Chloe This ain't jus' about me. I'm lookin' out for you. I'm tryin' to warn you. She's on her way. Bust her way in, break our necks.

Ivy I'm afraid I'm out of milk.

Chloe You're not bothered?

Ivy She might not come. Might not make it at all.

[*Offstage* **Boss**'*s bloodcurdling scream is heard from outside*]

Chloe What the … [**Chloe** *freezes. Her phone rings. She answers*] Yeah … ok ok … … calm down …

[**Ivy** *turns on the radio. It's the tune that has been heard before, evocative of weeds growing.* **Ivy** *hums along*]

Chloe What the … Is she okay? … Shit … Well waddaya want me to do? Okay … okay … [**She** *hangs up*] You'll never believe it. Boss was pelting along, all set to do us in. Something attacked her in the lift. Scratched her eyes out.

Ivy How shocking.

Chloe They've called an ambulance

Ivy Your coffee's getting cold.

Chloe You don't seem very surprised.

Ivy I thought you knew.

Chloe Knew what?

Ivy You spoke very clearly. I thought you knew what your words might do.

Chloe Wha' you chattin' about?

Ivy About words. Certain words.

Chloe You are messin' wi' my head. Repeatin' yerself.

Ivy Repeating's part of it. You must have noticed how everything repeats, the cycles of repetition. Anyway I thought you knew. But you say not?

Chloe Do you … know something?

Ivy It's you who knows … You … How can I phrase this? … You voiced your hate.

Chloe I like … *hexed* Boss?

Ivy You mean you cursed her?

Chloe Well, did I?

Ivy You seem to think I know everything.

Chloe This is all my fault, innit?

Ivy What do you want me to say?

Chloe What I mean is … I made this happen, didn't I?

Ivy Wasn't it an animal?

Chloe Yeah but maybe it was like … me.

Ivy Goodbye.

Chloe No, but … You gots explain this. 'snot fair otherwise?

Ivy Who said anything about fair?

Chloe But you gots explain de rules …

Ivy I'm afraid you're still confused.

Chloe [*sipping her coffee*] I've wished bad stuff on her like loads of time … it's never happened.

Ivy Ever told it to someone who listened?

Chloe Bin proper nasty in my head.

Ivy Well yes, sure. [**Chloe** *belches*] I tried to warn you – sometimes coffee reacts badly with that tea. The caffeine. [*The radio turns on of its own accord. It's the same tune, persistent*] Try to understand … the things you say … the things I hear … they're serious … powerful … actions, really … waiting to bloom … dormant … like seeds in winter … [**Chloe** *clutches her stomach*] You're wondering what we're going to do. We're not going to do anything. I've just got to give it time. Keep my eyes open, that's all. [**Chloe** *drops the cup*] Oh dear. [**Chloe** *starts to breathe heavily as the tune crescendos*] The truth is, none of this is personal. It's true that I've fantasised about a few things. The odd piece of nastiness for the odd nasty girl. But I've never wanted to make a point. [**Chloe** *dry wretches*] You don't seem to be grasping this. You don't seem to grasp that this is simply what happens. There's nothing anyone can do about it. I mean, what did you expect?

[**Chloe**'s *phone rings, beeps with a voicemail message, then beeps with a text. It begins to ring and beep with text and voicemail with increasing frequency.* **Ivy** *turns the music off*]

Chloe That'll be dem … Fuckin' hell … You knew Boss would get it.

Ivy I didn't.

Chloe You should've said.

Ivy Would that have helped?

Chloe You egged me on, you bitch.

Ivy Oh, I doubt you want to insult me.

Chloe You wanted this! You drugged me up, you made me say that thing, I knew you was a witch! [*As the texts, voicemails and phone calls reach a crescendo, the drilling of building work starts somewhere offstage*] I'm getting out of this death trap. Hand it over.

Ivy The flowers?

Chloe The fuck?

Ivy You were going to try and sell them?

Chloe The *fuck*?

Ivy For tea?

Chloe I was off my head! [**Chloe** *resumes her ransacking*]

Ivy We've been through this. I've got nothing.

Chloe Nothing, you say.

Ivy Nothing you would notice.

Chloe Why wouldn't I notice something?

[*Drilling and phone activity intensify*]

Chloe You sayin' I've missed something?

Ivy Would you like some more / tea?

Chloe No I fucking wouldn't.

Ivy Would you like / some?

Chloe How would I have missed something?

Ivy You wouldn't.

Chloe How?

Ivy How do I know what you have or haven't seen?

Chloe There's something here, isn't there?

Ivy I'm just an old woman, I don't know anything …

Chloe That kettle. Give.

Ivy Why?

Chloe [*taking the kettle*] I think you know … What have I missed?

Ivy Nothing, I told you … Or was there somewhere you didn't look properly? Yes, I think there was …

Chloe I've looked everywhere

Ivy Let me think, it'll come to me …

Chloe That's it, gimme your hands … [**Ivy**'s *fear escalates as* **Chloe** *holds the kettle over her hands*]

Ivy There!

Chloe Where?

Ivy There … there … where you just looked …

Chloe Where's that? Weren't notin' der, bitch.

Ivy It might be there now –

Chloe And why would it be there now?

Ivy It might be –

Chloe Money don't just *appear* now, does it? You best not be shittin' me … [**Chloe** *looks. She takes out the tin – it rattles with coins*] Fuck me. [*Opening it, counting out notes with relish*] £100 … £200 … £300 … £400 … £500 …

Ivy Take it.

Chloe Don't mind if I do. [**Chloe** *makes to leave. Then she stops, softens a little. She offers* **Ivy** *one of the fifties.* **Ivy** *shakes her head*] Don't be spastic.

Ivy No. Horrible stuff.

Chloe [*pocketing the money and walking to the door*] Should of give it me straight, shouldn't you?

Ivy I dislike being threatened.

Chloe Suit yourself. See you around. [**Chloe** *makes to leave*]

Ivy Hold on … [*Something in* **Ivy** *softens.* **Chloe** *halts*]

Chloe Yeah?

Ivy I've been waiting for you … Did you know that?

Chloe What?

Ivy Often I'm waiting … waiting for someone like you … I know you're coming … I'm wondering what I'm in for … a beating … or worse … And it makes me think – it's disgusting here – My life's disgusting –

Chloe So?

Ivy Would you let me finish?

[**Chloe** *waits*]

Ivy So I'm here in the cold, you're there with your threats – or worse – and I'm frightened – but not of you – not really – really, I'm worried – that you'll mess it up again, the way you always do … that they'll beat you up – that I'll see you – and to look at you lying there – will make me cry. [**Ivy** *waits until* **Chloe** *looks at her – is she fighting back tears?*] [*Understated but sincere*] But the thing that frightens me most – is what's happened already – you in my home – alone – pretending to be tough – your bluster – your hot air and attitude – us chatting and laughing – I can't change, you see – I'm not cut out for that – it's not in my nature – I can't – I can't – I can't look at you anymore.

[*Pause*]

Chloe Dat's de saddest ting I heard in my life.

[*There's a loud bang at the door*]

Boss [*offstage recording, from outside the door*] Bitch!

Chloe Oh my God …

Boss Bitch, I know you're in there?

[**Ivy** *appears disorientated. Drilling resumes, closer this time*]

Ivy Who's Bitch?

Chloe Shhh!

Ivy Is Bitch out there?

Chloe It's Boss, OK?

[*Drilling gets closer still. The door is being kicked from the outside*]

Ivy Boss? Are you Boss?

Boss [*offstage recording*] Bitch! Let me in, Bitch!

Chloe She's in hospital. How would she make it down here?

Ivy Who, Bitch?

Chloe *I'm* Bitch? [*A pipe bursts*] Shit ... [*Sound of something tapping its way away. Water continues to spew*] Just calm down, right.

Ivy I'm perfectly calm.

Chloe This is you, this is.

Ivy Excuse me?

Chloe Fuck! You made me ... make Boss ... come like dat Grudge ... from de *Grudge* ...

Ivy She's in hospital ...

Chloe I ain't thick! It's *connected*, innit? What you're feeling ...

Ivy Me?

Chloe *Does* stuff! Like ... like ... telekewhassit! Like *Carrie!*

Ivy Are we talking about films?

Chloe You get upset – *pipe bursts*!

Ivy Actually, I think it's the other way round.

Chloe What?

Ivy It's you. You're the one getting upset.

Chloe I am not!

[*The leak has stopped.* **Chloe** *calms herself down*]

Ivy Has it stopped?

[**Chloe***'s embarrassment at being soaking wet starts to show.* **Ivy** *looks at her*]

Chloe Look, have you got a shirt or what?

Ivy [*fetching a blouse*] Of course. Here.

Chloe You have got to be kidding me.

Ivy [*watching* **Chloe** *put the blouse on*] Suits you.

Chloe As if. [*Then birds begin chirping. It feels like dawn*] It were dinner time when I got here.

Ivy Was it?

Chloe Whas wi' de birds?

Ivy Birds like my flowers.

Chloe What time is it?

Ivy City birds. They can get confused.

Chloe [*checking the time on her phone*] Six a.m., my phone says.

Ivy So the birds are right.

Chloe I don't / get … (it)

Ivy Dawn. How lovely.

Chloe If you've done this …

Ivy Everything starting fresh.

Chloe I'll … I'll …

Ivy You'll what?

Chloe I'll kill you. [**Chloe** *sneezes*]

Ivy Well.

Chloe Well what?

[*The radio flicks on to a news report*]

Reporter Scientists believe that vegetation and wildlife could be adapting better than us to increasingly cold winters. Certain plants have become sturdier over the years, possibly due to increased pollution levels in our environment. A recent study suggests that new types called superstrains are on the rise. These take their name from their uncanny ability …/their uncanny ability … [*The radio repeats on a loop*]

Chloe It's as bad as you are!

Ivy Sorry?

Chloe Spraffing on – turn it off!

Ivy You do it. You're closer.

Chloe You turned it on.

Ivy I never touched it.

Chloe What?

Ivy It just does that sometimes.

Reporter And now for some breaking news … And now for some breaking news …

Chloe [*trying and failing to turn it off*] Fuck.

Reporter A teenage girl has been arrested this morning following an incident in the basement of a condemned building … A teenage girl has been arrested this morning following an incident in a condemned / building [*The radio repeats on a loop*]

Chloe Did you hear that?

Ivy What?

Chloe I'm gonna get arrested.

Ivy Really?

Chloe *I'm gonna get arrested!* [**Chloe** *is beside herself.* **Ivy** *turns the radio off*] You've got some explaining to do.

Ivy Have I?

Chloe You're making stuff happen …

Ivy I'm flattered.

Chloe You're making stuff happen to *me*!

[*Pause*]

Ivy If this is about the news report …

Chloe What about it?

Ivy If you're worried … about prophecy?

Chloe You use some proper stupid words. 'Prophecy'?

Ivy The girl on the news? She could be anybody.

Chloe F'real?

Ivy Of course … The police don't care what happens to me. I should know, I've called them often enough. Isn't that why you chose me?

Chloe How you make dem notes appear?

Ivy You miss what's under your nose.

Chloe … And de birds?

Ivy It's morning. Time passes.

Chloe I didn't notice.

Ivy Case in point.

[*Pause*]

Chloe [*starting to relax*] Right. Calm. Tanks, yeah?

Ivy You've nothing to thank me for.

Chloe Tanks for stopping Boss. Appreciate it.

Ivy I don't know what you mean. [*Pause*] You've got your money now. No one's shouting outside, nothing's bursting in here, no one can see your bra, nothing's falling down. So why the delay?

Chloe I … I'm …

Ivy I don't hear your 'friends,' if that's what you're worried about.

Chloe I'm sorry, OK? I won't be picking on you no more.

Ivy Well.

Chloe You've … you've made me tink … 'bout everting

Ivy That certainly was not my intention.

Chloe Don't matter, I owe you.

Ivy For what?

Chloe Wakin' me up? I'm gonna leave, das wha' I've decided – outta London, big flats council got out der. Gonna move, do some trainin', be a gardener, a gardener, right?

Ivy OK.

Chloe 'cos o'you. You like … inspired me, das wha' I'm saying. I wanted you to know that. Well?

Ivy No comment.

Chloe Do you mind if I put on the radio?

Ivy Suit yourself.

Chloe [*tuning the radio to something she likes*] I'm tryin' to tell you somefing.

Ivy I'm listening.

Chloe Dis is hard … When I tink 'bout Boss … Boss's lot … dem got notin' … *see* notin' … All de same … Not like you. [**Chloe***'s music develops a certain poignancy*] You got plants. Burstin' in through the ceiling. I get why you

Chloe (*cont.*) love 'em now – dem's feisty, like you. Shovin' in through that crummy concrete like it's cream cheese – fuck my sneezing, my hayfever – it's beautiful. Das how you see it, innit?

Ivy I suppose …

Chloe I know it is. An' what I'm sayin' is … I don't mind … powers an' dat … I'm sorry for freakin' out an' for … what I did to you … I was scared, I din't get it. But I do now.

Ivy Oh?

Chloe Being like you … It's like … an honour, ain't it?

Ivy If you say so.

Chloe You know it is. [**Chloe** *puts a hand on* **Ivy**'*s shoulder*] I should of taken more notice, I get dat now.

Ivy Makes no difference.

Chloe I should of … looked … I should of … noticed de *good* stuff.

Ivy Like what?

Chloe Life?

[**Ivy** *turns off the radio*]

Ivy [*suspicious*] I know what all this is about.

Chloe What?

Ivy 'The beautiful plants,' 'I love trees.' You still think I've cursed you, and you want me to take it back.

Chloe No …

Ivy You're scared, aren't you – you're more scared than ever!

Chloe Am not.

Ivy You heard the news on my decrepit radio. Some girl, some arrest. You can't let it go.

Chloe It's not like that.

Ivy Acting like you've undergone some kind of conversion. 'Sorry.' 'I love magical powers.' 'I really dig medieval witches.' You don't give a monkeys.

Chloe I do.

Ivy You only care about yourself.

Chloe I'm worried about you.

Ivy You're worried because murderers get life. [*Pause*] Admit it. You can't fool me, you know. It's better to admit it.

Chloe Alright maybe a bit … but I'd never get life … 'cos I never murdered you?

Ivy I wouldn't be so sure. You threatened me, dear. Held boiling water over my hands?

Chloe I didn't mean …

Ivy I rather think you did.

Chloe I weren't lyin', you know.

Ivy About what?

Chloe About likin' plants.

Ivy If you say so.

Chloe And flowers. And trees.

Ivy You really are breathtakingly stupid. Take some responsibility, young lady.

Chloe For what?

Ivy For everything. Everything that's broken.

Chloe What?

Ivy I'm saying, things are depraved.

Chloe Right.

Ivy Because of you, you swarming, multiplying 'bitches'; because of the horrors that made you and that you all made. You let that pack of feral animals abuse me –

Chloe Hang on, I / never … (did that)

Ivy You let them beat me 'til I couldn't feel.

Chloe What?

Ivy On and on. For decades. I had to suffer all that.

Chloe How old d'you tink I am?

Ivy You and the ones before. [**Ivy** *goes to the radio. She adjusts it back to its original station. It's her tune, the one* **Ivy** *hummed along to*]

Chloe I think you're a bit confused.

Ivy Let's change the subject, shall we?

Chloe [*listening to the music*] Dis was on before, innit? D'you like dis one? [*Tentatively, she moves to it*] Dis de beat, then?

Ivy Hardly.

[**Ivy** *watches* **Chloe** *trying and failing to find the music's rhythm. After a while,* **Ivy** *starts to sway. Then she takes* **Chloe**'s *hands. Soon they're both dancing*]

Chloe Gissa ya hand.

[**Chloe** *takes* **Ivy**'s *hand. On impulse,* **Chloe** *spins her round. Soon it's* **Ivy** *who's spinning her, further into her lair. They spin faster and faster. Suddenly,* **Chloe** *breaks free*]

Chloe Fuckin hell!

[**Ivy** *guffaws despite herself*]

Chloe You're mental, you are.

[**Ivy** *pulls herself together.* **Chloe** *laughs and pants.* **Ivy** *sits down.* **Chloe** *sits down next to her. She reaches out to a plant*]

Chloe What d'you call this, then?

Ivy You won't make me like you, young lady.

Chloe I'm interested.

Ivy Hedera. I told you.

Chloe What the fuck's that?

Ivy Ivy. You must have seen ivy.

Chloe Tell me about ivy. Then I'll go.

Ivy I don't believe you.

Chloe On my life.

Ivy What?

Chloe *On my life.*

[**Ivy** *considers this*]

Ivy Ivy has a scent. Not everyone notices; but it's there if you look for it. It's worth appreciating, I hope you agree?

Chloe Yeah. I do.

Ivy Liar. [*Beat*] You think all this is wretched.

Chloe No.

Ivy You think it's foul.

Chloe I like it. I told you.

Ivy I like it.

Chloe I know. Me too. [**Chloe** *breathes in the scent*]

Ivy Vines offer good insulation, you know. I like to sit right here with my ivy.

Chloe Me too.

Ivy Are you worried about coming any closer?

Chloe I'm not worried. [*The tune takes on a sinister quality as* **Chloe** *crawls up to the ivy, sticks her head right into it and inhales*] Wow, the smell. [*Breathing in vigorously*] That's intense, I'm … [**Chloe** *lies down in the ivy, fondling its tendrils. The sound and lighting grow disorientating*]

Ivy Hello? [*Beat*] Look, why aren't you moving? [*Beat*] Have you hurt yourself?

Chloe Watcha on about?

Ivy Your legs – are they damaged? Are they broken?

Chloe [*sitting up*] Course not … [**Chloe** *tries and fails to move her legs*] Pins and needles, tha's all. If you could jus' … [*reaching out with her hand*]

Ivy I'd rather not.

Chloe Jus' –

Ivy You got yourself into this mess, now you get yourself out.

[*The radio starts to crackle. Part of an Arts programme can be heard*]

Presenter [*intermittently fuzzy*] Orestes begs … Orestes begs … for mercy … but the Furies … the Furies … [*With a small bang, the radio cuts out*]

[**Chloe**'s *phone starts ringing*]

Chloe Could you pass me my phone, please?

Ivy I don't think so, no.

[*A voicemail message beeps*]

Ivy How long do the police take these days?

Chloe What?

Ivy They could be on their way.

Chloe Where?

Ivy Here of course.

Chloe My God, you grassed me up … [**Chloe** *starts to panic. She tries to stand up but her legs won't move*]

Ivy The ambulance may have notified them, I suppose. Boss's ambulance.

Chloe I … can't move – and the police …

Ivy Yes, the police investigate accidents. They might have a few questions.

[*A text message beeps*]

Chloe They're trying to warn me.

Ivy Are they?

Chloe [*trying to get the money out of her pocket*] Here –

Ivy Oh. That could look quite incriminating.

Chloe I'm trying –

Ivy Yes. In your pocket.

Chloe Take the money!

Ivy No thank you.

[**Chloe** *stops moving*]

Chloe What's 'incriminating'?

Ivy Bad. That money will look bad. In your pocket. Especially when I show them what you did to me.

Chloe Show them what?

Ivy My hands. [**Ivy** *holds out her hands*]

Chloe They're fine.

Ivy They're my livelihood. They're shaking.

Chloe No they ain't.

Ivy Shaking like leaves in the wind. Like wavering flames.

Chloe Jus' nerves.

Ivy Boiling water. It makes me nervous. It would make anyone nervous.

Chloe What are you saying?!

[*Another text and another*]

Ivy [*picking the phone up*] What an irritating invention. [**Ivy** *gives her the phone.* **Chloe** *opens the text message*]

Ivy Well?

Chloe Gonna throw Molotov. For Boss.

Ivy Why?

Chloe *For Boss.*

Ivy *Why?*

Chloe Start a fire? [**Chloe** *tries to get up and fails once more. She inspects the ivy.*] It's you, innit? [**Chloe** *grabs the vine*]

Ivy Don't be stupid.

Chloe Urgh. Got tentacles.

Ivy You mean tendrils.

Chloe I mean tentacles. Like an octopus. [**Chloe** *starts to crush the vine*] What the fuck! Get off me you bitch!

Ivy Don't do that. [**Chloe** *keeps crushing*] Dear, there are bees in your hair. [**Chloe** *thrashes around, trying to shake imaginary bees from her hair*] All gone. [**Chloe** *keeps thrashing*] I said, you can stop now.

Chloe I …

Ivy Stop fighting, you're making it worse.

Chloe I'm not, I … [**Chloe** *stops thrashing. She breathes in deeply. Then she gets up*] Oh.

Ivy You hurt her.

Chloe Sorry.

Ivy What are you waiting for?

Chloe [*looking at her afresh*] … You.

Ivy You are not.

Chloe I am.

Ivy Then you're more moronic than I thought.

Chloe I used to be.

Ivy What?

Chloe [*texting*] It's like dis. 'Fuck off. Mates.'

Ivy You insulted your friends?

Chloe Not friends. Cowards.

[*A Molotov cocktail is thrown from outside, smashing and bursting into flames not far away*]

Chloe We ain't got much time.

Ivy I have plenty of time.

Chloe Didn't you hear that? We need to get out of here.

Ivy I'm staying.

Chloe Don't be thick. [**Chloe** *grabs* **Ivy***'s arm.* **Ivy** *won't budge.* **Ivy** *is amused*] What's the joke?

Ivy No joke.

Chloe Well?

Ivy [*struggling to suppress her laughter*] It's you. Acting heroic. It's not appropriate.

Chloe Nah, I –

Ivy Are you trying to be a martyr?

Chloe Eh?

Ivy Unfortunately, the lady does not wish to be saved.

Chloe Is this a test? Like dat ting … dat stool in de lake ting … The witch drowned, didn't she?

Ivy Why the sudden interest?

Chloe It was a test, weren't it? And so is this!

Ivy Is it?

Chloe [*helping* **Ivy** *up*] Course it is, fam! Witches and fires, they burned witches – everyone knows that!

Ivy Listen …

Chloe *They burned witches.* But the real witch, does she like … magically survive? Come on, tell me how it works! [**Chloe** *leads them towards the door*]

Ivy I honestly couldn't say.

Chloe You don't like me. I'm not worthy, is dat it?

Ivy Would you like you?

[*Pause*]

Chloe Listen, I really am sorry. Not jus 'cos you might of hexed me. But 'cos I am. I wish you could believe me.

Ivy Thank you.

Chloe OK then.

[*A fire alarm goes off somewhere in the building*]

Ivy I never knew there were alarms …

[*The fire alarm stops*]

Chloe They treat me as bad as you, you know

[*Another two alarms go off*]

Chloe … I've got scars everywhere

Ivy So what?

Chloe I can't go back to that – leave, leave wi' me.

Ivy I don't do leaving.

Chloe Why the hell not?

[*More alarms gradually go off, increasingly malfunctioning*]

Ivy Listen, I'm old … I have to think of myself. I can't move, I can't uproot myself, I wouldn't make it.

Chloe You would. I'll help you.

Ivy No – I'm stronger alone. At home.

[*Pause*]

Chloe You're stayin' here. I don't believe it.

Ivy I am.

Chloe Burning though.

Ivy I can't fight any more.

[*The crackle of distant fire*]

Chloe I don't want you to die.

Ivy It's not up to you.

Chloe I can't jus' leave you, can I?

[*The radio turns on of its own accord. Again, the reporter repeats on a loop*]

Reporter A condemned building went up in flames today … A condemned building went up in flames today …

[**Chloe** *doesn't move*]

Ivy You look terrified.

Chloe Why ain't you shittin' it?

Ivy I'm prepared.

Chloe You're so calm …

Ivy I focus on details.

Chloe What?

Ivy Weren't you listening? … It's all backwards … out of sync … fuzzy …

Chloe Go on …

Ivy Flames, dying out … lungs puffing out smoke, fumes drifting away … bits of skin … uncurling … a tear racing up into an eye …

Chloe You're really fearless, aren't you?

Ivy I'm used to it, that's all.

[*Sporadically, the radio fuzzes*]

Ivy Fires like this one are nothing new … It started centuries ago for people like me … But the more they burned, the greater the fear … People were frightened, and that's what made the old hags strong … Weeds can flourish in the harshest conditions, did you know that?

Chloe [*sniffing the air*] There's a strange smell.

Ivy It's hate. Pure unadulterated hatred.

Chloe It's the plants. Are they toxic? Can you breathe?

Ivy Perfectly.

[*The smell gets stronger*]

Chloe [*counting out the money*] £100 … £200 … £300 … £400 … £500. Take it.

Ivy I told you. No.

Chloe It's yours.

Ivy Burn it. It's loveliest when it burns.

Chloe You burn it. Please.

[**Chloe** *crushes the money into* **Ivy**'s *hand. The crackle of flames grows louder*]

Ivy [*starting to hum her tune again*] I do like flames … waving in the wind … like beautiful orange leaves.

[*The shadows of the flames flicker as the fire approaches. A siren sounds*]

Ivy Just in time. [*Beat*] Well? I know what you want to ask, you know.

Chloe I gotta say it?

[*The siren comes closer*]

Chloe I don't blame you … I don't blame you for hating an' hexin' an' that, honestly I don't; I'm a hexer too … Ting is deep down, I know you're alright … 'cos you're like me … I know you are …

Ivy Spit it out, then.

[*Several vehicles pull up outside*]

Chloe [*summoning her courage*] Would you promise?

Ivy Promise what?

Chloe Promise I won't go down?

Ivy I promise.

[**Chloe**'s *gratitude is palpable. She hugs* **Ivy**]

Chloe Thank you.

Ivy [*reaching out she touches* **Chloe**'s *cheek tenderly*] You poor thing …

[*The doors of several vehicles open*]

Ivy It's the firemen. They're coming. [**Ivy** *opens a door to expose the fire*] I'm just going to sit here beside my ivy, dear. I'm just gonna catch my breath.

Chloe No time. You wanna act lively. [*Doors to the building slam open and shut*] Okay. Now move this way. They'll be here soon. [**Ivy** *moves towards the flames*] Here, there's an old lady here, I can't get her out! Hurry!

Ivy [*humming her tune she walks into the flames*] My hedera, but don't you look lovely. And I'm lovely. Your vines and my limbs, all burning together …

Chloe Oh my God. Can't you feel it?

Ivy It's a fusion … all mixed up …

Chloe You're in shock. Jus' –

Ivy This is the life, *this* is how it should be … [*As she burns on, weak*] Ow … perhaps I do need help.

Chloe Come back –

Ivy Is this it? Am I burning then? Oh … ow …

Chloe Give me your hand –

Ivy Come closer, dear …

Chloe Your hand – [*Sound of firemen approaching.*] Come on – [**Chloe** *moves to* **Ivy***, coughing more. She reaches out to* **Ivy***'s hand*] Here – [**Ivy** *coughs more*] Take it – [*Slight wobble as* **Chloe***'s hand makes contact with* **Ivy***'s*] No, don't – [**Chloe** *is pulled into the flames*]

[*Hand in hand, their eyes momentarily meet. Then* **Ivy** *lets go and slams the door on her.* **Chloe** *bangs and screams. There's a loud explosion.* **Ivy** *leans against the door, catching her breath*]

[*Exit* **Chloe**

[*Time passes*]

[*When the lights come up,* **Ivy***'s hair is down. Girlishly, she is twisting a dried flower decoratively into her hair. She stops at the sound of an approaching tap, tap, tap*]

Enter **Boss** *in dark glasses*

[*Her demeanour and clothes are much tougher than* **Chloe***'s. She makes slow progress, tapping her white stick,* **Ivy** *silently watching her*]

[**Ivy** *creeps towards her. Quietly, she leans towards* **Boss** *and brushes her face with the dried flower.* **Boss** *claws at her face, desperate to shoo off whatever was there*]

[**Ivy** *snorts with laughter despite herself*]

Boss [*pulling herself together*] Hello?

Ivy Ivy. They call me Ivy. Hello again.

Boss Have we met?

Ivy You're the leader. Top dog.

Boss You takin' de piss?

Ivy [*lighting her spliff and inhaling*] It's a vice, I know, but I do love to smoke.

[**Ivy** *proffers the joint, just out of reach.* **Boss** *inhales. Its potency hits her*]

Boss This is alright, innit.

Ivy I like it.

Boss Takes the edge off.

Ivy Are you feeling frightened?

Boss No.

[**Boss** *inhales. She starts to relax*]

Boss I thought if I faced it … faced de *fear* … [**Boss** *passes back the spliff*]

Ivy You poor thing … [**Ivy** *inhales*]

Boss So what we smokin'?

Ivy Bit of heliotrope, some Valerian. Perennials.

Boss What?

Ivy Plants that come back every year.

Boss [*spacing out*] Wow … like …

Ivy Reincarnation?

[**Boss** *sniffs the air*]

Ivy Weeds. Some of them flowering. [*Somewhere,* **Ivy**'s *tune starts to play*] They got burnt, of course. [**Boss** *starts to giggle.* **Ivy** *gives her a look.*] Fires aren't funny, you know.

Boss I know … I was jus' … I like dried flowers.

Ivy Oh?

Boss It's weird, why I like them … They kind of … live forever, if you get me?

Ivy Yes. I think I do.

[**Boss**'s *gaze locks with* **Ivy**'s*. *Ivy* looks back into her sightless eyes*]

Boss It's like they … never die … innit?

[*The tune fades out, the lights dim. In darkness, the sound of leaves rustling in the breeze*]